ROGUE'S PROGRESS

HARVARD STUDIES
IN COMPARATIVE LITERATURE

FOUNDED BY
WILLIAM HENRY SCHOFIELD

26

ROGUE'S PROGRESS

STUDIES IN THE PICARESQUE NOVEL

❧ ❧ ❧

BY ROBERT ALTER

HARVARD UNIVERSITY PRESS
CAMBRIDGE, MASSACHUSETTS

1964

FOR MY PARENTS

IN LOVE
AND GRATITUDE

PREFACE

THE COMPOUND title of this work may suggest a certain mildly schizophrenic note in the critical approach which has been adopted. After all, a "rogue's progress" implies that the picaresque tradition offers a very definite kind of archetypal figure who remains indubitably singular through all the plurality of embodiments in which we see him. "Studies in the picaresque novel," on the other hand, invites the inference that there is something random in the method of attack—either because the critic has avoided the problem of basic continuities, or because the subject matter itself is so amorphous that ultimately it resists definition. What I hope these chapters will show is that the apparently contradictory emphases of the title and subtitle are in fact dictated by the nature of the picaresque novel itself. There is, I believe, a genuine tradition of picaresque narrative which extends in space and time far beyond the borders of Renaissance Spain. Quite naturally, when the picaresque novel begins to cross national and temporal boundaries, it suffers many land and sea changes; so that while central continuities must be kept in sight, it is also important to realize that one encounters varieties of picaresque experience, and not simply *the* picaresque experience.

There is a curious polarity in the kind of attention that has been devoted to the picaresque novel. Literary scholars have been strictly specific and informative on the subject, while some literary critics of late have been highly un-

specific though occasionally suggestive. Between the two
lies a considerable stretch of terra incognita which deserves
exploration. The basic historical research on the picaresque
novel has already been carried out by a number of com-
petent scholars, and the present study will make no attempt to duplicate their work. The rise and development
of the picaresque novel in Spain have been examined
systematically by F. W. Chandler, Fonger De Haan, and
others. In a later book, Chandler attempts a comprehensive
description of the various kinds of roguish narratives in
English literature. An unpublished Harvard University
dissertation by Claudio Guillén carefully classifies the
varieties of earlier literature of roguery in order to deline-
ate precisely the emergence of the picaresque novel in
Spain as a new form. For all these writers, defining the
picaresque novel is a relatively straightforward task because they are dealing with a specific historical phenomenon. There can be no question that the picaresque novel is
a literary form that flourished in Spain in the latter part of
the sixteenth and in the first decades of the seventeenth
centuries; that it spread soon after to France, England,
Germany, Holland, and elsewhere; that it is the adventurous story of a rogue's life, usually told in the first person;
that its episodic account of wanderings, adversity, and
ingenious role-playing incorporates a satiric view of society.

In some recent criticism, on the other hand, there is a
tendency to see "picaresque" as a broad ahistorical category—like "comic," "tragic," "satiric," "bucolic"—which is
applicable to works of literature of all ages. As one might
suspect, writers who use the term this way differ considerably among themselves in what they mean by picaresque.
For some, it is merely a structural description: any episodic
novel-on-the-road is picaresque. For others, the term relates merely to the character of the protagonist, so that
any novel about a quasi-criminal wanderer or outsider is

picaresque. In this way, R. W. B. Lewis can consider such profoundly religious novels as *The Power and the Glory* and *Bread and Wine* as picaresque. Ihab Hassan is somewhat more cautious in using the term "neo-picaresque" to describe a group of contemporary American novels of existential quest. For a few writers, "picaro" is a pejorative, roughly synonymous with reprobate; for others, like Mr. Lewis, it is a word that can be applied to a saint. What each of these critics has done is to isolate a few elements from the traditional picaresque novel and to allow the part to come to stand in his mind for the whole.

There seems little point in using a term like "picaresque" without a sense of serious responsibility to the definite historical phenomenon from which the term derives. And yet I think there is a sound intuition behind these broader applications of the term, for it seems reasonable to assume that the picaresque novel is not simply a long-finished episode in Western literature but rather a permanent addition to the storehouse of literary resources, capable of regenerating and transforming itself in a surprising variety of new environments. As a delighted reader of picaresque novels, I began to wonder what there was in these books in particular which appealed so much to my imagination. What, I asked myself, is distinctive about the picaresque way of looking at the world? How does the writer organize his story and present his central character to reflect this distinctive vision? What distinguishes the picaroon's relationship with society from that of ordinary vagabonds, tricksters, outcasts, or criminals? Is there anything like a unique moral code implied by the peculiar picaresque mode of existence? To what extent are all such distinctive elements dependent upon the historical situation in which they were created?

With these large questions, and with a commensurate degree of trepidation, I approached the picaresque novel.

As far as possible, I have tried to make my method an inductive one. For this reason, I begin with the first example of the genre, *Lazarillo de Tormes*, though my main interest lies in the later developments of the picaresque novel, particularly in the eighteenth century. The brief consideration of *Lazarillo* seeks to discover some preliminary answers to the large generic questions, answers which will then be tested and amplified by an examination of the later picaresque novels. I discuss in considerable detail four eighteenth-century novels often referred to as picaresque in order to see what are the possibilities of picaresque experience, what is picaresque and what is not picaresque. By the latter part of the eighteenth century, literary sensibility and novelistic technique have evolved so far since the time of *Lazarillo* that it begins to be useful to talk, not about the picaresque novel, but about the transformations of the picaresque novel, or about picaresque elements in other kinds of novels. The final chapter attempts to explore a few of these new directions in which the picaresque novel has moved since the eighteenth century.

This inquiry into the inner nature of the picaresque clearly makes no pretense to comprehensiveness. The selective method adopted necessarily involves incompleteness; I have tried to keep it from involving distortion as well. If one does not care to be exhaustive, one should, I suppose, be at least suggestive. With whatever degree of success, that is what I have attempted to do in the chapters which follow.

This book began as a Harvard University doctoral dissertation in comparative literature, under the direction of Professor Harry Levin and Dr. Harold Martin. Though I have made some minor qualifications and amplifications, the present version is substantially the same as the dissertation. I am deeply grateful to Professor Levin and Dr. Martin, both for their knowing advice on matters large and small, and for their encouragement in urging me to follow my own idiosyncratic ways. It was a privilege for me to be guided by two such teachers. I would also like to thank Arthur Gold, now of Wellesley College, who read the finished dissertation and made a number of helpful suggestions for later revision. And I can only express a small part of my appreciation to my wife, who suffered through the proofreadings with me and in general has patiently put up with more picaresque everything than any nonprofessional would want to bargain for.

Robert Alter

New York
June 1963

CONTENTS

ROGUE'S PROGRESS

CHAPTER ONE

LAZARILLO AND THE PICARESQUE CODE

THE SECOND CHAPTER of *Lazarillo de Tormes* wastes no time in reducing the serving boy Lazaro to circumstances that inspire the courage—or rather, the inventiveness—of desperation. The hero of this anonymous little book, which in 1554 initiated the tradition of the picaresque novel, has left his first rapacious master only to find another just as grasping and distinctly more tight-fisted: from the stone pillar where he took ungentle leave of the blind beggar, Lazaro is tossed to a harder post with a village priest who pays him in starvation doles of shriveled onions. The miserly priest hoards all his provisions in an old trunk in the attic, making certain always to keep the key close about him, and while the trunk remains locked, little Lazaro wastes away. At a point when the penniless, homeless boy is beginning to envisage for himself an early grave, he discovers what the whole breed of his picaresque descendants will discover after him: that the incessant grinding of a stomach can sharpen the wits, and that famine, like fame, can move men to acts of daring.

And being in such affliction (God of his grace deliver every faithfull Christian from the like) not knowing how to counsell my selfe, my misery dayly increasing, upon a day, when by chaunce my wretched maister had gone abroad, there arrived by chance to the dore a tinker, which I believe was an Angel disguised, sente from God, who demaunded for worke: I answered softly, thou haste inough to amend in me, and I beleeve more than thou canst doe. But as it was no time then to delay the matter, (by divine inspiration) I saide unto him, uncle, I have loste the key of this coffer, I feare that my maister wil beate mee, for gods sake looke amongst your keyes if there be any that will open it, I wil consider your paines: the heavenly tinker began to assay, nowe one key, now another, of his great bunch, and I helped him with my prayers, so that immediatly before I was aware, he opened it: whereof I was so gladde, that mee thought I did see in figure, (as they say) the face of God, when I beheld the bread within it.[1]

What is remarkable in this passage—and elsewhere in the book—is the extent to which Lazaro introduces God, and His messengers, into the relation of his own roguish dealing. (All the references to the divine here in Rowland's version appear also in the original, with the single exception of the expletive "for gods sake," which is *por vuestra vida* in the Spanish.) Rowland apparently noticed the unusual attention Lazaro devotes to Providence, and following the 1561 French edition by Saugrin, he affixed an amusing marginal comment to the first sentence of our passage: "Lazaro was a good Christian believing that all goodnesse came from God." Lazaro, like some later picaroons, certainly talks like a good Christian, but we shall understand better in what kind of world this new figure finds himself if we consider just what kind of Christian he is—or can be.

Lazaro's namesake is, of course, not the resurrected Lazarus of John XI, but the indigent Lazarus of Luke XVI. The name itself is the Greek form of the Hebrew *Elazar*, meaning, "the Lord has helped." Lazarus, the sick, starving beggar in Luke, is very much in need of help from the Lord, for he gets none of it from his fellow men. Laid at the gate of the rich man, he is refused the crumbs he begs from the rich man's table, and only after death is he "helped" by God; angels come to carry him into Abraham's bosom. Under the traditional Christian view of the distribution of goods and the divine Distributor of goods,

Lazarus-Elazar is the proper name for a man who is destitute. If he is to escape in any way from his condition of misery, whether in this world or, as Luke has it, in the next, he must do it through God's help, since "all goodnesse came from God."

One does not have to follow Lazarillo de Tormes very far on his adventures to discover that he is not a Lazarus to let himself die of hunger by the gates of the unrelenting rich. If he concerns himself at all with the belief in a world to come, he is hardly prepared to suffer passively here and now and enjoy recompense only hereafter. As Lazaro learns about the world—for picaresque literature is very much a literature of learning, a literature of experience—he comes quickly to see in himself a creature that must be completely self-reliant if it is to get along in this world. Lazaro has a habit of summing up these "truths" of experience in aphoristic statements, and the statements are those of someone who knows he must help himself, and who has no compunctions about helping himself, because he realizes that there is no one else who will help him. This broad rule of action is the significant ethical implication of Claudio Guillén's generalization about the picaresque novel, "The basic situation of the picaresque novel is the solitude of its principal character in the world." [2]

So Lazaro, after having his head smashed against a stone bull by the blind man in his maiden experience with the great world, reflects, "My blind master hath good reason, it is ful time for me to open mine eyes, yea, and to provide and seeke mine owne advantage, considering that I am alone without any helpe." [3] (The Spanish here is somewhat more direct. "Verdad dice éste, que me cumple avivar el ojo y avisar, pues solo soy, y pensar cómo me sepa valer.") "This fellow says the truth," *this* is the truth for Lazaro: that he is alone in the world and must fend for himself. It is interesting that as soon as he is confronted again with his own absolute self-dependence, the phrase "to tell the truth" ("decir verdad") reappears. "And therefore to confesse the truth, if I had not found out means to helpe my selfe, I had bene buried long sithence." [4]

Now, for someone who has faced the hard fact of *solo soy* ("I am alone") so unflinchingly, it is particularly curious that Lazaro should have brought into the account of his meeting with the tinker: God the Father, the Holy Ghost, the Son of God (the bread which is God, the host), and an angel of the Lord—all within the space of less than twenty lines of print. A question immediately arises as to what tone was intended in these uses of the language of faith. When Lazaro describes his own shrewd resourcefulness as divine inspiration ("alumbrado por el Espíritu Santo"), does he seriously mean what he says, or is he trying to be ironic? It is temptingly easy to read ironies into a passage like the one we are examining, and it is more than likely that the author of *Lazarillo* meant us to perceive an ironic element in Lazaro's report of the incident, but it should be clear also that little Lazaro himself is innocent of ironic intention.[5] On the other hand, one would have to strain credence to the breaking point to assume that Lazaro is seriously convinced that the Holy Ghost has whispered instructions in his ear for robbing the parsimonious priest, or that the tinker was actually sent to him by the hand of the Lord (like the angels sent to Lazarus) to relieve him in his affliction.

The fact that the picaro can stand on a middle ground between the confidence of faith and the skepticism of irony is indicative of the peculiarly nonproblematic attitude that picaresque heroes take toward a distinctly problematic set of circumstances. Logically, if a man concludes that he is alone in the world, entirely dependent upon his own resourcefulness, it follows that he has effectively eliminated from the world any Providence that watches men's destinies and supplies their wants. The traditional hero is born into a world which has been waiting (often breathlessly) for his arrival. The anti-hero[6] —from Lazarillo's nativity one dark night by the River Tormes to the illegitimate birth of an Augie March in the ghetto of Chicago—finds himself dropped into a world as stolidly indifferent to his own existence as any absurd universe faced by the protagonist of an existentialist novel. But it is obvious that the picaroon, unlike the existentialist hero, is no philosophical prober: it never occurs to him to question the larger order of things. Though cast out into the world, and an outcast from society as well (in the sense that there is no place where he belongs in society), the picaroon is not a rebel—either against society, or against the traditional body of faith by which society explains the world order. Lazaro has not the slightest bent to pursue the radical implications of his own experience, or even of his own statements. Indeed, his progress depends upon the stability of the social hierarchy.

He lives in a world so thoroughly desacramentalized that the elements of the sacrament itself—bread and wine—appear with their religious significance turned inside out. Instead of a God who is the bread, bread becomes a God,[7] while wine, one of Lazaro's first objects of thievery, is the liquid with which the blind man so rudely baptizes him, prophetic of the day when Lazaro will make a living from wine, and live in the enjoyment of wine. ("Without doubt, Lazaro, thou arte more bounde to wine than thy father, for hee onely begot thee once, and it hath saved thy life a thousande times." [8]) Lazaro, in his actions, assumes this fact of a desacramentalized universe where hungry man pays obeisance to bread, not

God ("beholding the bread, which I durst not touch, but worshipping it" [9]), yet he does not trouble himself about the fact, or let the fact trouble him.

The sense of life which experience impresses upon Lazaro is a feeling of being tossed at random from event to event. The Spanish subtitle of *Lazarillo de Tormes* is *de sus fortunas y adversidas* (of his fortunes and adversities), and the words fortune, chance, fate occur frequently as Lazaro tells his story. Yet the picaro does not hesitate to mention chance and Providence in the same breath, as explanations of the same event: "There arrived by chance[10] to the dore a tinker, which I believe was an Angel disguised, sente from God." From a reader's point of view, Lazaro simply is guilty of a glaring self-contradiction, but Lazaro himself does not appear to be conscious of anything contradictory in what he has said. He is not in the habit of using words with indifference to their meaning, and it is worth considering how he can manage to juggle contradictory terms without being aware that they are mutually exclusive.

The picaresque imagination is peculiarly an imagination that can make out nothing beyond the scope of the status quo. No matter how often the picaroon suffers hearty kicks from the well-heeled boot of society, or from society's more down-at-the-heels footgear, he never begins to imagine a different, more equitable society, nor does he ever consider the possibility of rejecting society. And the same status quo imagination operates when the picaresque hero thinks at all of religion and religion's traditional articles of faith. People have always believed these things, and the picaroon sees no reason for questioning them. Golden-Rule Christianity and the predatory individualism of sixteenth-century Spain exist peacefully side by side in Lazarillo's mind, in direct contrast to Don Quixote. The one is a code which experience has taught him he must live by in order to get along. The other is a moral ideal that good Christians have always accepted —which is reason enough for the picaroon to accept it, which is reason enough, in fact, to eliminate for him the possibility of conceiving any substitute ideal.

Lazaro knows, like every faithful Christian, that the events of human life are all carefully ordered by Providence. He also knows that the events of his own life have swept him along in their tide and that, had he not learned to do some vigorous thrashing with his own arms and legs, the tide would have swept him under. His practical intuition of experience grasps it as an intersection of chance occurrences to be seized by the quick-witted individual for his advantage. But Lazaro makes no effort to match this intuition, which for him is empirically correct, against the belief in divine Providence, which for him is theoretically correct. The tinker stops at the house by chance: that is a fact of observation. But since Lazaro knows vaguely that things are supposed to be ordered by Providence—why should he suppose anything else?— he sees no difficulty in attributing the tinker's presence to the hand of God.

When the picaro speaks of the "heavenly" tinker (*angélico calderero*), an element of whimsy is at play in his choice of designation, mingled with a feeling that "Since such things may happen, then why not to me?" When he describes as divine inspiration his own divining of a plausible way to ask for a key, he is neither being ironic at his own expense nor making fun of revelation. Lazaro knows well enough that he has put to good use his own roguish inventiveness in his request to the tinker, but considering that the spirit of revelation is known to guide men in their trying hours, he feels he can assert without impiety that such guidance was vouchsafed him in his need. He is careful, however, not to make that assertion too gravely and not to attach too much importance to it.

The father of the picaresque tribe is, then, a good Christian in theory and a bad Christian in practice—which is to say, he is constrained to adapt himself to the demands of a thoroughly un-Christian world. But the revolutionary nature of his practical ethics is tempered by the fact that he is a traditionalist at heart. There are some values that he will continue to cherish even when experience might lead him to relinquish them. Ruthlessly pursued, the implications of the tangle of conniving and deception in which Lazaro finds himself would lead to a ruthless, tooth-and-nail code of behavior—of the sort one frequently finds in stage comedy. The initial encounter with the blind man offers an indication of this disturbing possibility. The traditional Judeo-Christian notion of how to act toward the blind, as toward all who are defenseless, is to protect them: its classic formulation is in Leviticus XIX.14. "Put not a stumbling-block before the blind." *Lazarillo's* blind man, however sightless, is far from defenseless. One might infer that in the sort of world he inhabits, he would have had to develop all his faculties of cunning and shrewdness to such a fine degree simply in order to survive. The blind beggar's rough treatment of Lazaro, moreover, finally provokes the boy to a literal reversal of the Biblical admonition: he places the blind before a stumbling block.

Lazaro demonstrates scarcely any compassion for his blind master, and the wily beggar himself gives little cause for compassion to be shown, yet even toward such a person, the picaroon's attitude does not altogether reflect an ethos of the jungle. The blind man, in all his hatefulness, remains a human being for Lazaro, not entirely an object to be trampled on, and Lazaro manages, at least in retrospect, to have some slight twinge of conscience over the way he dealt with his first master. He admittedly attributes this regret to the fact that subsequent events have proved the blind man was endowed with the gift of prophecy, but this is just another instance of Lazaro's half-whimsical theologizing of nontheological fact. His principal feeling toward the blind man is a kind of grudging gratitude, or at least recognition of service rendered; the blind beggar was the one who instructed him in the way of the world: "for next after God he made me a man, and although he was blinde, it was he that gave me sight and that taught mee howe to knowe the worlde." [11]

Fortunately, not all that Lazaro learns about life is included in the blind man's lessons on the need for cunning. That rigorous course of instruction could produce only the sort of individual who looks for the flash of the fang in every smile and the tightening of the prehensile paw in every handshake, while little Lazaro is just as inclined to see in his fellow man a fellow sufferer. Through his hardships the picaro discovers not only how to beg or steal the bread he is deprived of but what it means to be deprived of bread. This faculty for empathy with other human beings in need prevents the picaroon from being radically alone in his world; it keeps him from following to its end the predatory code which can be derived from his awareness of his absolute dependence on himself. It is this faculty for empathy that provides the chief motive in Lazarillo's behavior toward the squire. Lazaro has nothing to gain from the squire; had gain been his object, he would have done better to have left the indigent *hidalgo* as soon as he discovered how empty his larder was. Lazaro, however, is susceptible to other feelings. "God take suche compassion on mee, as I did then uppon him for I had oftentimes endured, yea and daily felt that sorrow, which I knew tormented him: wherefore . . . I wished that the poore man wold have eased his paine, by helpe of mine, and that he wold have eaten with me for company." [12]

At one extreme, Lazaro's experience-hardened individualism can reach such a degree of self-centeredness that he blithely imagines God killing off parishioners so that he, the hungry servant of the parish priest, can enjoy the funeral feasts. But Lazaro also proves himself capable of compassion, and, as his comment on his action toward the squire suggests, he connects this compassion with a sense—fundamentally a religious sense—of his own human imperfection. The picaro in practice may improvise his own rules of permissible conduct, yet he does not conclude that his personal will is the sole standard by which he is to be judged. "I answered softly [so that he would not hear me],[13] thou haste inough to amend in me, and I beleeve more than thou canst doe."

It is the distinctive nature of the picaresque hero to be an image of human solitude in the world and at the same time an image of human solidarity in the world. He travels alone and struggles alone, for he finds that he can rely only on himself. Experience teaches him to regard other people with suspicion, and he discovers it is useful—often indispensable—to follow this principle in his dealings with men. Yet he does not question the rightness of the more generous attitude toward others that is prescribed by Christianity, and his familiarity with the pangs of an empty stomach suggests to him that there are other human beings just as needful of Christian charity as he. The picaresque hero in this way is a figure both detached from the society of men and possessing a profound sense of involvement in the human condition. The vantage point gained by this double nature of the picaroon offered a new, broader perspective to the narrative art in which society and the individual could be seen.

CHAPTER TWO

THE INCORRUPTIBILITY
OF THE PICARESQUE HERO

IN THE EIGHTH BOOK of Lesage's *Gil Blas,* the gay-spirit-
ed picaroon from Santillane is forced to give an account of
his past to the Duke of Lerma, first minister of Spain.
Gil Blas does his best to glide over the more incriminating
details of his eventful career, but he cannot keep the Duke
from perceiving the truth.

> Monsieur de Santillane, me dit-il en souriant à la fin de mon
> récit, à ce que je vois, vous avez été tant soit peu *picaro.*
> Monseigneur, lui répondis-je en rougissant, Votre Excellence
> m'a ordonné d'avoir de la sincérité; je lui ai obéi. Je t'en sais
> bon gré, répliqua-t-il. Va, mon enfant, tu en es quitte à bon
> marché: je m'étonne que le mauvais exemple ne t'ait pas
> entièrement perdu. Combien y a-t-il d'honnêtes gens qui
> deviendraient de grands fripons, si la fortune les mettait aux
> mêmes épreuves! [1]

> ("Monsieur de Santillane," he said to me smiling at the end
> of my account, "from what I can see, you have been a little bit
> of a picaro." "Monseigneur," I answered him blushing, "Your
> Excellency ordered me to be honest, and I obeyed him." "I am
> pleased with you for it," he replied. "Never mind, my boy,
> you've come out of it cheaply: I am astonished that bad example
> has not entirely ruined you. How many respectable people are
> there who would have become perfect scoundrels if fortune
> put them to the same test!")[2]

The Duke of Lerma's comment to Gil Blas in fact
raises a major question about the nature of the picaresque
hero: though the picaroon is usually no better than he
should be, it is really surprising, in view of the tests to

which experience puts him, that he is not worse than he
actually is. The model of Lazarillo suggests one answer
to the question. The picaroon may have natural inclina-
tions toward roguery, but he is not by nature a scoundrel.
Though his scruples of conscience are few and faint, he
demonstrates some strength in the virtues of the heart.
Gil Blas, like Lazarillo de Tormes, is disposed to compassion for his fellow men. Characteristically, in his first
important encounter with the misfortune of others, he
describes his response to a fair lady's tears. "Je pleurai
même aussi, tant il est naturel de s'intéresser pour les
malheureux." [3] ("I myself cried as well, so natural is it
to feel concern for the unfortunate.")

But this particular element of the picaro's moral make-
up should not be overstressed in explaining the fact of his
picaresque incorruptibility. If we push such an explanation
too far, we are liable to find that our picaroon has un-
expectedly become a kind of ne'er-do-well Christ. (This,
as a matter of fact, is what R. W. B. Lewis has done in
his recent collection of essays, *The Picaresque Saint*. The
picaroon is, after all, a rogue—a tough-minded individualist in a harshly competitive world, and one may wonder
how useful a definition of the term picaresque is when it
has been so broadened that it can include a series of
manifestly Christ-like figures.) Gil Blas is clearly a more
complex creature than Lazarillo, and in the case of
Lesage's picaroon, it is in the anti-hero's distance from
men, not in his solidarity with them, that the main clue
to his incorruptibility is to be sought.

Any consideration of the character of Gil Blas must,
of course, take into account the complicating circum-
stance of Lesage's authorial intervention in the figure
of his protagonist. Even in the first part of the novel, it
is clear that Gil Blas is not quite a bona fide picaroon, at
least not in the manner of the earlier, simpler Spanish

narratives of roguery. The youthful vagabond from the country town of Santillane is caused to say things and make observations one could scarcely expect from him: Lesage uses the picaroon to a great extent as his own satirical vehicle. At the same time, in this first-person narrative the author also maintains a careful satiric distance between himself and his protagonist. But while Lesage's intervention qualifies the character of Gil Blas, the picaro is clearly more than a tool for the author. His speech and action and thought as he pursues his career fall together into the configuration of a consistent and distinctive personality, and one which is well worth examining.

There is an unfortunate tradition in the French criticism of Lesage that has one easy explanation for Gil Blas's resistance to the immoral world in which he lives: Gil Blas was thought up by a Frenchman, a fact which in itself is enough to make him more moral than any picaro conceived by a scurrilous Spaniard. The line of critics who have adopted this position runs from Ferdinand Brunetière to Maurice Bardon, but it reached its apogee a generation ago in Gustave Lanson,[4] who went so far as to assert that anything artistically bad or morally reprehensible in *Gil Blas* was Spanish, while anything in the novel morally or artistically admirable had a French source.

It is highly questionable whether any valid general distinction in moral stature can be made between the Spanish and the French picaroons. One would feel easier about having Gil Blas over for tea with the best spoons out than one could be with Guzman d'Alfarache, but Guzman in any case represents the far end of the picaresque spectrum bordering on villainy, and Spanish Lazarillo as well as French Gil Blas looks virtuous beside the doubtful scion of the stock of Alfarache. These French critics are right, however, about one aspect of Gil Blas:

the French-speaking version of the Spanish picaro is more French than his Spanish predecessors. Now, if we avoid equating French with high-mindedness and unswerving virtue, we may discover that what stamps Gil Blas with telltale Gallic features despite his Spanish garb is also what chiefly determines how he acts toward men and in what ways he will not be corrupted by them.

The two great French influences on Lesage, as many critics have noted, were Molière and La Bruyère. The linking of these two names to Lesage's underlines the obvious fact that the author of *Gil Blas* is a conscious satirist, but it should suggest something more specific about Lesage's particular habits of mind and eye, and, consequently, about the habits of observation of his first-person narrator and hero, Gil Blas. All satire involves an element of distance between the writer-observer and the world which is the object of his observation. In order to see what is absurd or reprehensible in the ways of men, the satirist must take a few steps backward to a vantage point from which he can survey the field. The general coloring of the satire will depend to a large extent on how great this satiric distance is. If the writer is very close to his object of observation, as in the case of a Dos Passos or a Samuel Butler II, the satire is likely to have a dense emotional atmosphere. If the writer puts himself at a great distance from what he observes, as is true of satirists like Voltaire and Swift, men appear as a swarm of minuscule creatures falling into a neat intellectual pattern imposed by the mind of the satirist. Molière and La Bruyère stand on a middle ground between these two extremes of satirical perspective. They place themselves far enough away from the society they scrutinize to observe it with a degree of emotional detachment and to discern general patterns in its behavior, but they are close enough to be capable of a minute and precise observation of manners and morals.

Gil Blas is a moralist in the same sense the term can be applied to Molière and La Bruyère (and his method more clearly follows that of La Bruyère)—which is to say, he is a critical observer of *moeurs*. This habit of observation is a faculty which characterizes Lesage's hero from the beginning of his career. Because it tends to keep one segment of Gil Blas's awareness apart from the world in which he is involved, it prevents him from ever being dragged body and soul into the Way of the World.

The detachment of the satirist-moralist is not an absolutely necessary characteristic of the picaresque hero, but it is a stance easy to adopt in the picaresque situation, and one which is particularly natural for the French picaroon to take. If the picaro rejected society or rebelled against it, if he took to the hills instead of to the road, he would not be interested in society's workings or in its corruptions. If, on the other hand, he had a fixed place in society and made its goals identical with his own, he would no longer have the perspective to see what is wrong in and with society.

In connection with the inherent satirical perspective of the picaresque situation, it is especially significant that the picaroon is a servant of many masters. He will not let the social system pin him down; mobility is part of his essential nature; but he willingly accepts a position of subservience within the social system. This submission to servitude is an aspect of the picaresque hero which is not likely to sit well with the modern reader. According to our notions, a man, particularly a man who is the subject of a novel, ought to be his own master. One has to keep in mind, of course, that the picaresque novel was born in the sixteenth century and flourished in the seventeenth and eighteenth centuries in a society which, however fluid by comparison with the Middle Ages, still preserved a strong sense of social hierarchy. Gil Blas is not a Rastignac or a Julien Sorel. He may do considerable squirming around and even climbing up the social heap, but he never doubts that those who are at the top of the heap belong there because they were born there, and, consequently, he is not really trying to "arrive." Conversely, the nobleman, because of his noble nature, cannot become a picaroon: the fugitive Don Alphonse watches the horses while Gil Blas, Don Raphaël, and Ambroise go off to gull a moneylender, but Lesage will not let his aristocrat participate in an act of roguery.

The picaroon, then, accepts servitude because his imagination does not suggest the possibility of radically altering his original place in the social scheme. But there is a positive as well as a negative reason for his willingness to become a servant. The servant's position offers him the opportunity both to observe and to take advantage of society without being concerned with many of the demands that society makes on the individuals belonging to it. Servitude implies, among other things, irresponsibility. The picaroon takes what he can from others, but he does not have to take care of his own because he never collects the various kinds of baggage of his "own" which would encumber him. Servitude allows him in this way to be his own master in fact, though not in form, as he could not be were he to take a "respectable" place in society. It is this appealing element of the servant's place that Fabrice stresses when he first convinces Gil Blas to become a valet: half a century later, this very conception of the calling will be carried out brilliantly by Beaumarchais' Figaro.

> Le métier de laquais est pénible, je l'avoue, pour un imbécile; mais il n'a que des charmes pour un garçon d'esprit. Un génie

supérieur qui se met en condition ne fait pas son service matériellement comme un nigaud. Il entre dans une maison pour commander plutôt que pour servir. Il commence par étudier son maître: il se prête à ses défauts, gagne sa confiance, et le mène ensuite par la nez.[5]

(The lackey's calling is burdensome, I admit, for a simpleton, but it has only charms for a fellow with wits. A superior spirit who puts himself in service does not simply do his job like a fool. He enters a house in order to command rather than to serve. He begins by studying his master: he lends himself to his faults, wins his confidence, and afterwards leads him by the nose.)

The acceptance of the lowness of servitude has one noteworthy moral corollary: the picaroon must surrender a good part of the general human desire to appear important in the eyes of others. By voluntarily becoming a serving man he retires from the general scramble for status and respect and puts himself in a position to survey that scramble with great clarity. This is why the adventuress Lucinde's remark to her son Don Raphaël represents a distinctive picaroon's-eye view of the world: "Voilà le monde! chacun s'imagine être au-dessus de son voisin." [6] ("That's the world! everyone imagines himself to be above his neighbor.")

The picaroon's location, therefore, in the midst of the social system without being altogether part of it, is an invitation for him to turn satirist. He will be more likely to take up the invitation when, as is the case for Gil Blas in contrast to Lazarillo de Tormes, the struggle for the necessities of daily existence is not so grimly pressing. And his satirical comments will take on a particularly Gallic flavor if he has the zest for language, for the finely turned epigram, for the stroke of wit, that we discover in Gil Blas.

It has become a kind of ritual in discussing Gil Blas's use of language to cite the statement that the Count of

Olivarès makes in Book XI about the remarkable naturalness of Gil Blas's style. Perhaps more to the point is a
comment made much earlier in the novel by Gil Blas
himself in his role as the worthy disciple of the homicidal
Dr. Sangrado. Dr. Cuchillo, a suspicious and able rival,
has just emphatically expressed his "faith" in the competence of his youthful colleague. Cuchillo's remark leaves
Gil Blas doubtful and a little uneasy. "Il dit cela d'un air
si naturel, que je ne savais s'il avait parlé sérieusement,
ou s'il s'était mocqué de moi." [7] ("He said that with such
a natural air that I didn't know whether he had spoken
seriously or whether he was mocking me.") These same
words could be applied to a large part of Gil Blas's relation
of his own adventures. For the satirical distance between
him and his world expresses itself characteristically in
irony. And it is not Gil Blas alone who is an ironist in this
novel. There is a whole cast of picaroons than Lesage works
into his narrative—Fabrice Nuñez, Diego Pérès, Laure,
Don Raphaël, Scipion[8]—and as each one takes the center
of the stage to tell his own story, we are presented a
world seen through the eyes of a habitual ironist.

Irony, when it appears as such a persistent mode of
discourse, is a good deal more than a rhetorical device.
It is an attitude of mind, a way of seeing the world and
relating to the world. Just what this way is for Lesage's
hero will become clear from considering a few specific
examples of the use of irony in *Gil Blas*.

The first extended adventure of the cavalier of Santillane is his imprisonment in the bandits' cave. The young
would-be scholar finds himself hopelessly trapped in a
dark cavern, at the mercy of a group of thieves, com-
manded to serve table under the supervision of a witchlike
old cook. The circumstances are enough to crush anyone
not cast in the indestructible temper of heroes, and Gil
Blas, picaroon that he is, freely admits that he is forged

from much more fragile material. Yet misfortune does not overwhelm him. "Je cédai à la nécessité, puisque mon mauvais sort le voulait ainsi; et dévorant ma douleur, je me préparai à servir ces honnêtes gens." [9] ("I yielded to necessity, since my evil fate so willed it, and restraining my sorrow, I prepared myself to serve these good folk.") Apart from the obvious ironic intention in the final phrase, there exists both here and throughout the episode an explicit irony in the contrast between the elegance of the style and the crudity of the situation.

At first glance, it seems remarkable that Gil Blas can demonstrate in such a predicament a resilience that even allows him to be capable of irony, but perhaps it would be more accurate to say that the habit of irony is what makes him capable of such resilience. Gil Blas is not entirely the bewildered adolescent trapped in the cave. If he were, the cave would frighten him much more, as, for example, Fagin's den frightens Oliver Twist once that much simpler lad realizes into whose cruel clutches he has fallen. There is a more knowing Gil Blas that hovers above the Gil Blas involved in the experience and sees the experience in a broader perspective. It is this knowing Gil Blas who can address comments about the bandits over their heads to an audience as knowing as he, who can refer to the thieves ironically as "ces honnêtes gens." It is his sophisticated scrutiny-from-above of Captain Rolando and his men that has the effect of reducing them to papier-mâché desperadoes in a make-believe Hades.

As part of his ironist's strategy of converting the terrible into the comical, or, at any rate, of rising above his dilemma, Gil Blas translates the whole cave episode into the language of mythology. Léonarde, the haggish cook is described as "ce bel ange des ténèbres" (that lovely angel of the shadows).[10] Gil Blas reports his installation as waiter to the thieves in the following terms: "C'était la

señora Léonarde qui avait l'honneur de présenter le nectar
à ces dieux infernaux, ils la privèrent de ce glorieux emploi
pour m'en revêtir. Ainsi, nouveau Ganymède, je succèdai
à cette vielle Hébé." [11] ("It was Senora Leonarde who
had the honor of presenting the nectar to these infernal
gods; they deprived her of that glorious office to invest
me with it. Thus, a new Ganymede, I succeeded this vener-
able Hebe.") The windings of the darkened cave make
it a "new labyrinth" for Gil Blas, and Domingo, the vigil-
ant Negro guard, is inevitably a "Cerberus" whom a
hundred Orpheus-flutes could not succeed in charming.
(We might recall that later it is a good dose of rheuma-
tism and gout which averts the watchful eyes of Domingo.)

There are admittedly points in the novel where mytho-
logical references are merely an automatic—and sometimes inappropriate—rhetorical gesture, but Lesage more
often uses myth with ironic intention, and the scene in
the robbers' den is certainly an instance of such intention.
By superimposing the grandeur of the gods on an assem-
bly that is an underworld only in the modern sense of
the word, Gil Blas succeeds in reducing even murdering
thieves to nearly comic stature. This ironist's way of
looking at things keeps experience—even when it is threatening—at arm's length, and prevents it from totally sub-
merging the picaroon.

The distancing of immediate experience is not the only
significant advantage of Gil Blas's stance of irony. As
important as the fact that Gil Blas can step back from
the people whom he encounters in his adventures is the
fact that he can step out of himself to look at himself
from an ironist's perspective. Here is how he describes
his own descent into the highwaymen's underworld: "Les
cavaliers m'y firent entrer avec eux; puis, baissant la
trappe avec des cordes qui y étaient attachées pour cet

effet, voilà le digne neveu de mon oncle Perez pris comme un rat dans un ratière." [12] ("The horsemen made me go in with them; then, lowering the trap door with ropes which were attached to it for that purpose, there was the worthy nephew of my Uncle Perez, caught like a rat in a rat trap.") Lesage handles the ironic thrust of this sentence with great skill. First he explains the mechanics of entering the cave in a prose rhythm, dangling a long participial phrase which he cuts off sharply with the immediacy of "voilà"; then the rhythm tightens to the regularity of verse as Gil Blas detours to introduce the deftly ironic self-designation, followed by a caesura, and then the final banging-down of "pris comme un rat dans une ratière."

The most important redeeming trait in Gil Blas is this ability of his to look at himself as if he were someone else; it prevents him from taking himself too seriously, it enables him to see what is ridiculous in himself as clearly as he would see it in others. Much has been written about the marvelous gaiety of Lesage's picaresque hero, but it is chiefly Gil Blas's freedom from solemnity about himself that is responsible for his gaiety. Two brief examples should give some idea of Gil Blas's distinctive trick of stepping outside of Gil Blas.

On the second page of the novel, the picaroon describes his litigiousness as an eager young student in Santillane. This is how he sees himself:

Je m'appliquai aussi à la logique, qui m'apprit à raisonner beaucoup. J'aimais tant la dispute, que j'arrêtais les passants, connus ou inconnus, pour leur proposer des arguments. Je m'addressais quelquefois à des figures hibernoises qui ne demandaient pas mieux, et il fallait alors nous voir disputer! Quels gestes! quelles grimaces! quelles contorsions! Nos yeux étaient pleins de fureur, et nos bouches écumantes; on nous devait plutôt prendre pour des possédés que pour des philosophes.[13]

(I also applied myself to logic, which taught me to reason

much. I became so enamored of disputation that I would stop passers-by, whether I knew them or not, in order to propose arguments to them. I sometimes addressed myself to Hibernian personages who asked for nothing better, and then one should have seen us dispute! What gestures! What grimaces! What contortions! Our eyes were filled with furor, our mouths foamed; one would have sooner taken us for madmen than for philosophers.)

The final pointed contrast between the rational ideal of the debaters ("philosophes") and the unbridled emotionalism of the debate ("possédés") is indicative of the sharp satiric perspective in which Lesage's hero can view himself.

The Gallic picaresque gaiety—which Gil Blas shares with Fabrice, Diego Pérès, Laure, and Scipion among his picaresque companions in this novel—emerges distinctly as the concomitant of the picaroon's awareness of his own absurdity when he describes his professional debut in full medical regalia.

En sortant de la maison du pâtissier, je rencontrai Fabrice, que je n'avais point vu depuis la mort du licencié Sedillo. Il me regarda longtemps avec surprise; puis il se mit à rire de toute sa force, en se tenant les côtés. Ce n'était pas sans raison; j'avais un manteau qui trainait à terre, avec un pourpoint et un haut-de-chausses quatre fois plus longs et plus larges qu'il me fallait. Je pouvais passer pour une figure originale et grotesque. Je le laissai s'épanouir la rate, non sans être tenté de suivre son exemple; mais je me contraignis, pour garder le *decorum* dans la rue, et mieux contrefaire le médecin, qui n'est pas un animal risible.[14]

(Upon leaving the baker's house, I met Fabrice, whom I had not seen at all since the death of the licentiate Sedillo. He looked at me a long time with surprise; then he began to laugh with all his might, holding his sides. It was not without cause: I had a cloak which dragged along the ground with a doublet and hose four times longer and wider than I needed. I could have passed for an original and grotesque figure. I let him enjoy his hearty laugh, not without being tempted to follow his example; but I restrained myself, in order to preserve decorum in the street, and to better counterfeit the doctor, who is not a risible animal.)

There is one important moral consequence to the fact that Gil Blas's satirical scrutiny can be turned on himself as well as on others. Lesage's hero clearly recognizes himself as part of the fellowship of fools that comprises the human race. In this respect, his literary ancestry goes back beyond French classicism to Erasmus and Rabelais. He points out the absurdities of mankind's follies, but he does not rant against them: his ironies are not bitter or cynical. All this is to say that the picaresque sense of solidarity with mankind is strong in Gil Blas, however much he is a satirical observer and however much he has a sharp eye out for his own profit.

But what is especially interesting is the indication that his faculty for compassion is continuous with his satirical consciousness; the fact that irony is at play is no proof that sympathy has been withdrawn. The picaroon is no sentimentalist, and sometimes the satirical quip will even be his way of expressing sympathy and distress for human suffering. This is what is behind Gil Blas's comment in Book VII on the penniless amputee officer; only superficially does his remark appear to have achieved cleverness at the expense of being cruel. "Ce que j'admirai dans les relations de batailles et de sièges qu'il me fit, c'est qu'il ne lui échappa aucun trait de fanfaron, pas un mot à sa louange, quoique je lui eusse volontiers pardonné de vanter la moitié qui lui restait de lui-même pour se dédommager de la perte de l'autre." [15] ("What I admired in the accounts of battles and sieges he gave me was that he allowed no touch of bragging to escape him, not a word in his own praise, although I would have gladly pardoned his vaunting the half of him he had left to compensate himself for the loss of the other half.")

These two attitudes, then, which one might expect to be
at odds with each other—the satirical perception of human
absurdities and the sense of fellowship with humanity—
coincide in the picaresque world of *Gil Blas*. Nowhere is
this happy coincidence more strikingly illustrated than in
Gil Blas's encounter on the road with Melchior Zapata, the
wandering thespian who is reduced to indigence by his
wife's unreasonable and unprofitable virtue.[16] Gil Blas and
his friend Diego Pérès discover Zapata in the shade of a
roadside grove, soaking in a fountain the hardened crusts
of bread which are all his provision. The young actor
laughingly invites the two newcomers to join him in his
meal, and they readily agree, on condition that he will
allow them to add some items from their own stock to the
common menu. The three travelers enjoy a pleasant hour
of companionship (they literally "share bread" in this experience of fellowship), deploring the adamant virtue of
pretty young wives and bemoaning the precarious fate of
all those whose calling it is to tread the boards. After the
meal, Zapata starts down the road, gesticulating and de-
claiming as he goes. Gil Blas and Diego are quick to pick
up their cue, and they answer the actor's performance with
a barrage of hisses and catcalls in the best manner of
Zapata's Madrid audiences. Zapata turns, believing himself
for a moment back at the scene of his recent theatrical
fiasco, but when he realizes that the hisses are only the
invention of his new acquaintances, he himself bursts into
laughter and continues down the road, laughing his way
out of sight.

This episode of wanderers' companionship should indicate how far the picaresque code can depart from the code
of a literary form to which, on first thought, one might
expect it to be closely allied—stage comedy. Lesage, like
many novelists, was first a playwright and then a writer of
fiction. In 1709, just six years before the appearance of the

first part of *Gil Blas*, Lesage wrote his best-known play, the satirical comedy *Turcaret*. It is instructive to consider how the code by which the personages of *Turcaret* guide their actions differs from the picaresque code implied in *Gil Blas*.

Lesage's play is clearly in the tradition of "hard" comedy exemplified by Machiavelli's *Mandragola* and Ben Jonson's *Volpone*. Under any kind of scrutiny, the world of *Turcaret* proves a very unpleasant place in which to be. Nearly everybody in *Turcaret* is a scoundrel. There is not even the usual division between the cheater and the cheated, for the most badly deceived characters turn out to be victimizing someone else just as ruthlessly as they themselves are victimized. In this world, virtue is simply the ability to be sharper than the next fellow, and love is no more than a temporary blindness that renders one vulnerable to the keen-fanged wolves prowling on every side. The picaresque code insists on a similar need to be sharp and self-seeking, but the picaresque qualities of compassion, companionship, affectionate good humor, are totally unimaginable in the world of *Turcaret*.

Since there is no evidence to warrant any assumption that Lesage had a crucial change of heart between 1709 and 1715, it seems likely that the reason for the disparity between the codes of *Turcaret* and of *Gil Blas* lies in the difference of genres. Most human beings are probably inclined to conduct their lives on the presupposition that there really is such a thing as human affection (which, because it is affection, has an element of disinterestedness in it) and that human fellowship is not entirely illusory. But along with this hopeful view of humanity, we carry the awareness that many of the people we encounter seem to act largely on motives of pure self-interest. This contradictory awareness has been embodied in the convention of stage comedy, or a main tradition of it, where peo-

ple—viewed wholly externally—are assumed to be moti-
vated invariably by self-interest. A convention of this sort,
however effective on stage, does not lend itself very
readily to a first-person novel form.

One of the reasons that the picaroon always tells his
own story is in order to close the distance between him
and his reader.[17] This low-life, homeless, rag-clad rogue
is also a man like you, hypocritical reader, his double, his
brother. If he steals, it is because he needs what he takes,
or because he is following the impulse that is latent in
all of us to put himself outside the restraint of the law—
but not because he is vicious through and through. A
reader will not find it easy to put up with the "hero" of
a long narrative who proves to be an absolutely unmitigated scoundrel—or to speak more precisely, the reader
will not be able to identify with him. This is the problem
Fielding runs into in his quasi-picaresque novel *Jonathan
Wild*. Fielding could not possibly have used a first-person
narrative, even were it his practice; his anti-hero had to
be attacked completely from the outside. The result is a
remarkable feat of sustained irony, but it can become a
little irritating to read after a while precisely because it
is a novel in which there is no possibility of sympathy, no
opportunity for identification.

The novel, by allowing us to know its people more
intimately than we can know the people we meet in daily
life, helps to broaden our range of moral awareness and
to strengthen our sympathies with kinds of human beings
that—at least superficially—are alien to us. The picaresque
narrator consequently must be more than a soliloquizing
Volpone. If his rogue's autobiography is to do more than
simply assault the reader's moral sensibilities, there must
be something of the gregarious beast underneath the
wolf's clothing, something of the risible animal inside the
hard-minded schemer.

We have seen how Gil Blas's most human qualities are directly connected with the satiric distance between him and mankind (and between him and himself). It is by virtue of this distance, this perspective, that the picaroon can join in the corrupt activities of society and not be corrupted radically by them. Gil Blas may be "supple to the point of meanness," as Eugene Lintilhac has written, but his moral pliancy never really collapses into baseness precisely because he is also—as Lintilhac goes on to say— "everywhere and always an observer." [18]

In this connection it is worth recalling the major instance in the first part of Lesage's novel in which Gil Blas consciously resists an environment that threatens to debauch him. In the closing section of Book III, the picaroon obtains a position as a servant in the establishment of Arsénie, a coquettish fashionable comedienne. At first his head is turned by the glittering life of theater people and their followers, but he soon becomes disgusted with the vices of the actors' society, and he decides that he had best take quick leave of Arsénie. At the beginning of the next book, Gil Blas explains his sudden departure to the steward of his former master. "Après avoir demeuré près d'un mois chez Arsénie, dont les moeurs ne me convenaient point, je venais d'en sortir de mon propre mouvement pour sauver mon innocence." [19] ("After having stayed nearly a month at Arsénie's, whose way of living in no way suited me, I have just left on my own initiative in order to save my innocence.") Maurice Bardon comments in a note on the word "innocence"—"Is Gil Blas making fun of himself or of the person to whom he is talking?" [20] Gil Blas clearly has an ironic awareness of the contrast between his own actual state and innocence, but it seems to me that M. Bardon misses the paradoxical appropriateness of the term that our picaroon has chosen for himself. Though one would hardly apply the word "innocent" to Gil Blas in the same way it is used for dimple-cheeked cherubs and little girls in first communion dresses, he does possess a genuine innocence that the world cannot subvert.

We must be careful, of course, to distinguish in fiction between the kind of innocence which is a serious part of characterization and that innocence which is merely the product of literary convention. The protagonists of some novels—particularly when they are first-person narrators—exhibit a curious narrative innocence that has nothing to do with the experiences they undergo: Sade's *Justine* preserves a scrupulous virginity through all the nightmare of wild orgies and bestial degradation to which she is subjected. In the case of *Gil Blas,* however, it would appear that Lesage has converted a picaresque convention of narrative innocence into an element of genuine characterization. Gil Blas's limited but significant virtue is not simply the result of an authorial fiat, for it is consistent with his character as presented in the novel and with the way we see him exercise his calling of picaroon.

After enumerating to himself the vices that permeate the atmosphere of Arsénie's household, Gil Blas concludes, "Je ne veux pas demeurer plus longtemps avec les sept péchés mortels." [21] ("I don't want to stay any longer with the seven deadly sins.") The picaroon in effect is calling our attention to an innocence which he can justly claim. Gil Blas does not pretend to any great moral punctiliousness, but every one of the Seven Deadly Sins is essentially foreign to his picaresque nature. As a man of many talents who has chosen the humbleness of the servant's place in order to get along in the world, the picaro is innocent of the sins of Pride and Envy. Though he is always on the lookout for new means—whether honorable or not—to replenish his personal stock, the amassing of riches never becomes an end in itself for him, and we could hardly accuse him of Avarice. A subtle manipulator of men who must ingratiate himself with them, he could not permit himself the luxury of Anger. While he has hearty natural appetites that he is not embarrassed to satisfy, he cannot, as a man who lives by his agility, get entangled in the snares of sensualism: Gluttony and Lust have no place in a picaresque career. And it goes without saying that a figure who embodies protean enterprise and quick-witted opportunism will in no way be guilty of the sin of Sloth.

It would appear, therefore, that the unique nature of the picaroon's vocation armors him against the world's corrupting influences, or at least against those vices that involve meanness of soul or a crippling of the healthy will. And the segment of awareness in the anti-hero that continually views experience from a satirical distance safeguards him against being lured out of his picaresque immunity into the moral quicksands which surround him. It is this kind of awareness that makes Gil Blas realize what he has got himself into in Arsénie's employ and why he must get out "in order to save his innocence."

An apparent difficulty in this whole idea of picaresque incorruptibility is the fact that it is blatantly contradicted by what happens in Books VIII and IX of *Gil Blas*. Once Gil Blas has become part of the court life at Madrid as confidential secretary to the Duke of Lerma, he does just what the picaroon is supposed not to do—he succumbs to all the corrosive influences around him. In fact, he is soon tainted with the very vices whose contagion he had avoided by fleeing the household of Arsénie. As the powerful secretary of the most powerful official in Spain, Gil Blas becomes avaricious with a vengeance, proud and envious, and for the first time capable of anger. Lesage's hero, with his characteristic gift of conciseness, gives us a fine description of his change from picaro to the sort of personage that could step right into the cast of characters of *Turcaret*.

Avant que je fusse à la cour, j'étais compatissant et charitable de mon naturel; mais on n'a plus là de faiblesse humaine, et j'y devins plus dur qu'un caillou. Je me guéris aussi par conséquent de ma sensibilité pour mes amis; je me dépouillai de toute affection pour eux.[22]

(Before I came to court, I was compassionate and charitable by nature; but at court one no longer has human weaknesses, and I became there harder than stone. I also consequently cured myself of my sensibility toward my friends; I stripped myself of all affection for them.)

Even the distinctive buoyant gaiety of this Gallic picaroon is lost in the relentless effort of self-seeking that the court imposes on him. "L'avarice et l'ambition qui me possédaient changèrent entièrement mon humeur. Je perdis toute ma gaieté." ("The avarice and ambition which possessed me entirely changed my nature. I lost all my gayness.") And as Fabrice succinctly puts it to the picaro, "Enfin, Gil Blas n'est plus ce même Gil Blas que j'ai connu."[23] ("In short, Gil Blas is no longer the same Gil Blas I knew.")

The picaroon, in other words, is no longer a picaroon, or, to transfer Fabrice's observation to the problem of literary classification, the picaresque novel, when it reaches a point like this, has metamorphosed into something other than a picaresque novel. The narrative, to be sure, retrospectively maintains its distance from this vice-ridden sometime picaro, but the relevant point is that the principal actor of the narrative has become in this section quite different from the fellow he once was.

Wherever we encounter him, the picaroon appears as a fixed personality who never substantially alters during the course of his varied experiences. He learns, but he does not change. In the early chapters of a picaresque novel, the young hero is generally made to undergo some sort of *déniaisement* or "wising-up." Gil Blas has five or six such experiences in Book I before his education is complete. This same ritual of initiation is practiced in the novels of Balzac, Stendhal, and in the *Bildungsroman* in general, but in these works it is the first step in a process of serious inner development. The picaroon, on the other hand, once he has learned all the rules of the game—and particularly what are the special hazards of the game—goes on to play with skill and confidence, but nothing has happened to him inside, no development has taken place.

The picaresque novel is a form of narrative which is concerned with action and the external world. The tension or "conflict" that keeps this narrative taut is the individual's incessant and ingenious struggle to take a livelihood from a grudging world. As the picaresque novel moves away from its Spanish origins, the stress tends to be more on the ingenuity and less on the struggle. The events and motions of this struggle are the principal interest; not the personality of the struggler, which is never even highly particularized. We are allowed to see the world through the eyes of a moderately interesting and believable individual, but it is the world that we are supposed to see, not *his* world; he—his inner life, his psychological complexity, his moral growth or decline— is not allowed to come between us and the large world. So the picaroon is, of necessity, a fixed, undeveloping character.

It is also true, however, that the picaresque novel, like so many things, bears within it the seeds of its own transformation. One of the chief innovations of the picaresque narrative was to make the narrated episodes pivot upon a "real" individual—real because he was an anti-heroic hero, a plebeian, a resourceful but limited human being who had to face the human problem of getting food in his stomach and, if feasible, a roof over his head. Once this innovation had been made, it was a natural temptation for the author to begin concerning himself with the individual personality of this real individual at the center of the episodic narrative. In this way a modern novelistic interest in character emerged from the narration of adventures, and the fixed features of the protagonist began to relax, revealing a creature susceptible of serious development.

Such a process is clearly at work in *Gil Blas*. The picaresque novel of 1715 has become, in its 1724 sequel, a kind of narrative that is only residually picaresque and that is already very close to the *Bildungsroman*.[24] For Lesage's hero is made to undergo a radical transformation of character. First, as we have seen, he is completely corrupted by the court, changed into a very different person from the picaroon he once was. Then his sudden imprisonment drives him to the depths of despair; gone is the picaresque resilience of his earlier cave imprisonment; in his misery he even becomes introspective (Book IX, Chapter V). Finally, after a bout with a classic case of symbolically significant near-fatal illness, Gil Blas becomes a new man, touched by contrition, endowed with a "perfect tranquillity of spirit" and a new, reflective view of life. The use of prison confinement as a symbolic womb for the hero's rebirth looks forward to Stendhal. The link between Lesage and the great nineteenth-century novelist of the self-conscious—and developing—individual should indicate how far this section of *Gil Blas* has come from pure picaresque narrative.

The shift in focus from the man's adventures to the man himself is accompanied by a change in the tempo of narration. The episodic nature of the picaresque novel is a function of the picaroon's fixed character. Because the picaroon has the ability to "wake up every morning as though it were the first day of his life," [25] as Erich Auerbach has said of the Homeric hero, he encounters experience as a series of episodes, that is, a succession of more or less self-contained units in which there is no necessary sequence. When Lesage begins to describe a process of development in his protagonist, the episodes that previously comprised his narrative visibly merge into a single continuum. Books VIII and IX, with the exception of the two interpolated stories of Don Roger de Rada and Don Gaston de Cogollos, constitute one continuous progression, beginning with Gil Blas's moral decline in court, reaching a crisis in his "conversion" in prison, and arriving at a final resolution in the ex-picaroon's amendment of wrongs to his parents and his Horatian retirement to the country house at Lirias.

In general, it is not surprising that a novelist should want to add some sort of post-picaresque stage to his picaro's career. If he does not resort to the post-picaresque, he involves himself in a serious technical difficulty: there is no way of ending a picaresque novel. It is with considerable justice that Gines de Passamonte retorts to Don Quixote's question on the completion of his rogue's autobiography, "How can it be finished, my life being not yet ended?" [26] All you can readily do with a picaresque novel is to break it off and leave it deliberately in a to-be-continued state, for its episodic structure affords no natural point of conclusion. Picaresque novels have always invited sequels. If one was not forthcoming from the original author, there were often other writers only too willing to pick up the thread of narrative where it had been left dangling. It is a tribute to Lesage's novelistic insight that he discovered something more creative to do with his hero than merely to settle him down at the end of his adventures. The picaroon, scapegrace though he may be, is also, like the traditional hero, a child of the gods: despite all the troubles he gets himself into, he is never seriously hurt and never perceptibly tainted. In *Gil Blas*, Lesage has given us both the imaginative pleasure of following such a happily protected creature through his adventures, and an interesting consideration of what may happen to this hero as a man when his picaresque immunity has worn off.

CHAPTER THREE

A BOURGEOIS PICAROON

IT IS SCARCELY surprising to discover that a woman who makes a trade out of love can be as harsh of mouth and as tough of mind as she is easy of virtue. But Defoe's Moll Flanders has, after all, the advantage of early and extended contact with gentility, and it remains her great ambition to be a proper gentlewoman. If circumstances eventually lead her to walk the streets, she still feels that she really should be sitting in respectable homes, and she scrupulously avoids the language, the mannerisms, and the ways of thinking of the gutter. In any case, Moll's outspokenness and her ability to be tough-minded have something peculiar about them; a close consideration of these qualities in the Newgate-born lady of fortune may lead to a more precise understanding of her distinctive attitude toward the world.

Defoe assures us in the preface that his anti-heroine "is made to tell her own tale in modester words than she told it at first." [1] About one thing Moll's account of her career of sin is indeed almost chastely reticent. She usually manages to skirt the physical act by which she makes her way in the world with some stratagem of euphemism or circumlocution. "I by little and little yielded to everything, so that, in a word, he did what he pleased with me; I need say no more." [2]

Her husbands and lovers never lie with her, but "offer her a kindness in that way," "offer something of that kind," or "go to that which they call the last favor." At best, Moll simply fits her illicit unions into a general moral category without designating their particular nature; characteristically, she describes her amours with the older brother of her foster family as "our crime" and "our wicked pleasure." Though this kind of genteel euphemism is a familiar convention in English criminal biographies, there is good reason to suppose that its use in *Moll Flanders* represents an important step toward the realistic employment of language for characterization. A strong sense of reserve about sexual matters is, as we shall see, entirely consistent with Moll's whole mental make-up.

But what makes this degree of reticence in Moll somewhat surprising is the contrasting brutal frankness of which she is capable. When, for example, the anti-heroine wants to tell us that her incestuous marriage with her American husband is physically disgusting to her, she minces no words. "Everything added to make cohabiting with him the most nauseous thing to me in the world; and I think verily it was come to such a height, that I could almost as willingly have embraced a dog as have let him offer anything of that kind to me, for which reason I could not bear the thoughts of coming between the sheets with him." [3]

Defoe's would-be gentlewoman, in spite of her own frequent resort to euphemism about sexual matters, has a habit of cutting sharply through all camouflaging phraseology and rapping out harsh realities in the short, unambiguous syllables of what she herself calls "plain English." Thus she sums up the career of a thieving couple with which she briefly collaborated: "She was not his wife, but they were partners, it seems, in the trade they carried on, and partners in something else. In short, they robbed together, lay together, were taken together, and at last were hanged together." She treats an insidious proposal from the old governess in the same vigorously candid fashion. "She said something that looked as if she could help me off with my burthen sooner, if I was willing; or, in English, that she could give me something to make me miscarry." Moll is just as quick to give the most unambiguous name to a chief source of the governess' income. " 'Tis scarce credible what practice she had, as well abroad as at home, and yet all upon the private account, or, in plain English, the whoring account." [4]

It is worth noting, moreover, that these moments of unmitigated candor in Moll are by no means limited to her judgments of other people. She is just as ready to put the plainest label of condemnation on her own actions. When, for example, the politic governess tells pregnant Moll, "You must e'en do as other conscientious mothers have done before you," Moll at once makes the appropriate unspoken observation. "I understood what she meant by conscientious mothers; she would have said conscientious whores." [5] Moll's unflinching honesty with herself reveals itself very clearly in an exchange with her first seducer. The wanton young gentleman, after half a year of intimate relations with Moll, has suggested that she marry his brother.

"But here, my dear," says he, ". . . you shall always have my respect, and my sincere affection; . . . you shall be my dear sister, as now you are my dear—" and there he stopped.

"Your dear whore," says I, "you would have said if you had gone on, and you might as well have said; but I understand you." [6]

It is tempting to conclude that all these instances of frankness in Defoe's anti-heroine reflect an admirable— and particularly picaresque—kind of candor. The picaroon in general is an individual who does not act according to "official" morality because, observing how such morality is more frequently preached than practiced, he realizes that he must ignore much of it in order to get along in the world. Since he has no set place in society and is not committed to the established order, he is free from the tribute of lip service to conventional morality which most people feel is exacted from them. He can call a thief a thief and a whore a whore, even when he is the thief or his wife is the whore.

But the case is quite different with Moll Flanders. Her candor, as I shall try to show, derives from a highly unpicaresque source. It is a kind of candor, we might note at the outset, that extends over only one part of her experience. Far more significant than Moll's moments of reticence is a real failure of conscience—certainly from a picaresque viewpoint—in the account she gives of her life. The tough-minded honesty that made her insist on the appellation "whore" when she deserved it all but evaporates after Moll and her Lancastershire husband settle in America with a stock of capital accumulated from prostitution, shoplifting, housebreaking, pickpocketing, and armed robbery on the road. Her perfunctory twinge of conscience over the source of the wealth is quickly overcome by the sense of well-being in finally setting up a comfortable, respectable, and dependably profitable establishment.

The fact is that Moll is not nearly so witheringly honest with herself as some of her moments of frankness might lead one to conclude. Moll's creator, of course, was not only a journalist-novelist but also a steadfast Dissenter, and he may well be speaking sincerely when he asserts in the preface that his book is meant "to discourage and expose all sorts of vice and corruption of manners." [7] This moralist's impulse in Defoe partly explains why his lady of fame is made to call herself bluntly by the name her actions earn her. Moll, a Puritan in all but virtue, generally shies away from words that evoke the physical actuality of her polygamies and prostitutions, but she shows no hesitancy in branding herself a whore because it is a word that is used not so much to describe as to denounce, not to call forth an image but to affirm a stern moral judgment. What, then, has happened to the rigorous moralist when this mistress of many thieving trades arrives at her happy ending, tranquil in mind with the accumulated profits of years of crime?

The disparity between the anti-heroine's vigorous self-condemnation in the main body of the novel and her surprisingly easy conscience at the end of the book offers only an apparent contradiction. It is not really true that Moll is harder on herself as a practitioner of love for profit than as a retired thief. The language is harsher when she speaks of her amorous misdeeds, but her self-condemnation remains a superficial one. And there is a reason for this harshness of language which is quite distinct from the moralist's ends that Defoe may have felt he was realizing.

Moll's propensity for plain-dealing words is in fact directly connected with one peculiar habit of speech that appears with almost annoying frequency in the course of her narration. She repeatedly tacks onto nouns of a certain kind qualifying explanations introduced by phrases like "that is to say," "as I called him," "as it is called." The various characters, for example, who have some kind of dual or false identity in the novel are continually referred to with the addition of such explanatory phrases. When Moll goes on her trip to Lancastershire with the young lady who later proves to be a swindler, Moll, as narrator, cannot conceal her retrospective awareness of the false identity of those involved in the plan to swindle her. "Well, I went with my friend, as I called her, into Lancastershire"; "Her uncle, as she called him, sent a coach and four horses for us." "My friend, who called him brother . . ." An adopted bastard in the house of Moll's accomplice and mentor must be described as "my governess's grandchild, as she called her." Once Moll has discovered that her American husband is also her brother, she does not hesitate to make the forbidden duality of their relationship painfully explicit. "I was now fully resolved to go up point-blank to my brother (husband)." [8]

In general, Moll is uncomfortable using any word whose referent is not altogether clear and unambiguous to her. So she describes a storm on her voyage home from America, "The ship sprung her mainmast, as they called it." Moll, on her part, is not sure exactly what a mainmast is, and she will not take responsibility for the word. This desire for perfect clarity leads her to a suspicion of all figurative language. In the rare instances when she slips into using a metaphor, she is quick to explain its literal meaning or at least to apologize for using it. "This he took for a favor, and so laid down the cudgels, that is to say, the pen." "In the sixty-first year of my age, I launched out into a new world, as I may call it." [9]

The significance of this stylistic habit may become clearer when we recall a memorable figure in English literature before Moll who had a similar mannerism. Shakespeare's Jew of Venice, like Defoe's lady of Newgate, mistrusts the imagination and the language of metaphor that pertains to the imagination. "Water-thieves and land-thieves," he says to Bassanio, and then quickly explains, "I mean pirates." Later he warns Jessica to "stop up my house's ears, I mean my casements." [10] Moll and Shylock are both outsiders, and in the case of each this habit of speech may reflect, at least in part, the speaker's sense of not belonging to the world of which he speaks. (The picaroon, on the other hand, is an outsider who generally manages to feel at home in his world.) Moreover, Shylock's suspicion of the poetic is as characteristic of his mercantile bent as it is of his outsider's unsureness, and we may infer from the curious parallel between Shylock and Moll that her own attitude toward the imagination and toward the uses of language is very much on the side of the moneylenders.

By contrast, a kind of nimbleness of imagination is a fairly constant component of the picaresque make-up; it is what endows the picaroon with the lightness of heart that wins our affections as well as with the inventiveness that enables him to lighten his neighbor's pockets. Moll Flanders, on the other hand, apart from rare moments of brightness like her first relationship with Jemmy, is anything but lighthearted. A real, red-blooded picaro, in the style of Lazarillo de Tormes or Gil Blas, is a man of imagination by calling. Born in—or rather outside of—a hierarchical society where each individual is assigned a fixed place, he can envisage for himself the possibility of assuming multiple roles. Life is not for him a cut-and-dried product which the buyer must accept exactly as it is handed him, but rather a plastic material which the artistic individual can shape in any of numerous ways. The picaroon has no difficulty in imagining something which can participate in more than one identity at the same time—as witness Lazarillo's angelic tinker and Gil Blas's netherworld highwaymen. His manner of conceiving things is frequently metaphoric because he has a keen awareness of the potential multiplicity of the nature of things.

Moll Flanders, however, insists on living in a world of cold, hard facts. She likes reality to stand still—so that it can be counted—not to shimmer, not to flow from one identity to another, not to comprehend, even for a fleeting moment, a thing and its opposite. The contrast between her kind of mind and that mentality which is characteristically picaresque is reflected in the different attitudes the two take toward disguise. In premodern society, clothing was not only decorative and protective, but had a very definite and important emblematic function. The garment was a clear and fixed symbol of class and calling. The picaroon, in escaping from the fixity of the social system, inevitably becomes a quick-change artist with a large and varied wardrobe. He not only uses disguise adeptly for highly practical purposes, but—as is true for most comic characters—the activity of disguise is something in which he delights. In slipping off one costume and putting on another, he affirms his protean nature, he achieves a sense of the broad range of possibilities of what he, the picaroon, can be.

Moll Flanders, on the other hand, remains wholly Moll Flanders even when the exigencies of her career in thieving lead her to go out in disguise. Putting on different clothes does not mean for her putting on a new identity, or even playing a new role. She is in fact as uncomfortable with the idea that Moll Flanders can be anyone else, as she is with the idea that an adopted girl can be the governess' "grandchild," or that Jemmy's fellow conspirator is his "sister." It is instructive to note that the two disguises in which Moll feels most uneasy—almost guilty— are a man's clothes and a beggar's rags. Of the various costumes she puts on, these are the two which most contradict her own fixed nature; the one denies her sex, the other her constant need to preserve personal propriety. In the latter case, she is literally punished for descending so far from herself: she gets no profit from it, and she resolves never to resort to such a low disguise again. Interestingly, Shylock, Moll's literal-minded mercantile predecessor, is as much at a loss as she in the face of exchanged identities; he is finally undone by a woman playing a man's role with consummate skill.

Defoe's quasi-picaresque heroine is, in the last analysis, a very serious businesswoman. She cannot cope with a complex, multiple, contradictory reality; she must break it down into counters that have clear and unequivocal values stamped on their faces. She calls a whore a whore not so much out of moral honesty as out of moral literalmindedness. She will not let people ease an act out of the straightforward, unambiguous category in which she has been taught it belongs: you either are or you aren't, and—rather than suffer the faintest uneasiness of doubt— Moll is quick to say that she is.

This anti-heroine's tough-mindedness, in sum, is largely a result of her literal-mindedness. At several points in the narrative, her handling of language clearly suggests the close connection between these two qualities. Early in the novel, when the younger brother of Moll's foster family becomes enamored of her, the mother begins to show some animosity toward the parish child that she has taken into her home. "In short, his mother had let fall some speeches, as if she intended to put me out of family; that is, in English, to turn me out of doors." [11] Moll tears away the veil of euphemism because she wants to name the thing plainly and exactly by its right name, and a necessary concomitant to her verbal literalism is a moral literalism. She insists on the blunt phrase for what Robin's mother wants to do, and consequently she faces the unadorned harshness of the mother's intentions toward her.

One further example should suffice to illustrate the point. When the "widowed" anti-heroine takes up residence in the Mint and puts herself on display in the usedwife market, she soon discovers to her dismay that financial assets are the only assets of a woman which are really in demand. "Being well-bred, handsome, witty, modest, and agreeable, all of which I had allowed to my character, whether justly or no is not to the purpose; I say, all these would not do without the dross. In short, the widow, they said, had no money." [12] Moll reflects her own discomfort with the world's periphrastic manner of putting

things and looking at things in the hesitant and awkward
first sentence, so different from her usual swiftness and
trimness of style. Then she rejects the implied metaphor
—virtue as gold, money as dross—and insists on the literalism—gold as gold—in a terse summation, sharply stressing
the short, plain words she uses. "The widow, they said,
had no money." When Moll impatiently cuts across the
coils of circumlocution to get at the hard core of literal
meaning, she also slices through the hedging and evasions
of the prospective husbands to confront the undisguised
self-interest that motivates them.

I have already suggested, in noting the connection with
Shylock, that this aversion to things disguised, to metaphor and to paradox, is related to a typically mercantile
way of looking at the world. The precise nature of this
relationship is implicit in one of the central ideas enunci-
ated by Max Weber in his classic analysis of the capitalist
mentality. Weber repeatedly argues that what distinguishes modern capitalism from traditional orientations
toward the world is its insistence on converting all economic pursuits, indeed, all of life, into radically rational
activity. Weber uses "rational" in a rather special sense.

Everything is done in terms of balances: at the beginning
of the enterprise an initial balance, before every individual
decision a calculation to ascertain its profitableness, and at the
end a final balance to ascertain how much profit has been
made . . . So far as the transactions are rational, calculation
underlies every single action.

Later in his book, Weber contrasts this attitude toward
gain with that of older forms of economic activity.

It is one of the fundamental characteristics of an individualistic capitalistic economy that it is rationalized on the basis of
rigorous calculation, directed with foresight and caution toward
the economic success which is sought in sharp contrast to the
hand-to-mouth existence of the peasant, and to the privileged

traditionalism of the guild craftsman and of the adventurers' capitalism, oriented to the exploitation of political opportunities and irrational speculation.[13]

It is not surprising that Weber cites Defoe twice as a significant spokesman for the new capitalism. And capitalist rationalism, as Weber describes it, is the characteristic that permeates all the thinking and all the actions of Moll Flanders. In true capitalist—and Puritan—fashion, she conceives everything she does in terms of a rigorous system of bookkeeping.[14] It is for this reason that she expects words to be used with neat, very definite denotations unobfuscated by any suggestion of multiple meaning or contradiction. In an account book, after all, one works exclusively with numbers: each listing has a precise, unvarying value, and the bookkeeper can always know exactly in what state his affairs are simply by totaling the figures. That is why it is unsettling for Moll to deal with terms which will not stand still the way numbers do, which threaten to shift value or to have more than one value at once.

E. A. Baker, in his *History of the English Novel*, has recognized that *Moll Flanders* is a picaresque novel only in its surface qualities, though it seems to me that he offers a rather misleading idea of what kind of book it really is. "Except in its autobiographical procedure, incidents succeeding each other with the chance disconnexion of real life, there is nothing of the picaresque in *Moll Flanders*. The heroine is a rogue, but not one rejoicing in her rogueries. To the modern reader, her life is a serious study of the effects of heredity and environment in the making of criminals." [15]

The last suggestion can be dismissed as a somewhat unfortunate lapse in historical perspective. There is no point in trying to make Defoe into a kind of eighteenth-century Zola. If he has some rudimentary notions of social and hereditary causes for crime, they are considerably more primitive than the modern conceptions first fully articulated in the nineteenth century, and they are certainly not the central concern of his novels.

What is more instructive in Baker's comment is his observation that Moll is no picaroon because she is a rogue who does not rejoice in her rogueries. The picaro engages in a variety of cheating practices in order to obtain money, but it is never solely in order to obtain money. It would be an exaggeration to say that the picaroon is indifferent to money: he views it as the wherewithal he must have to satisfy his needs and desires, and therefore the more of it he can get, the better off he is. But money does not become for him the single consuming end to which all means are subservient. The picaroon does delight in his rogueries for their own sake. They are for him not only a means of making profit, but a magnificent game affording an opportunity for the exercise of art and ingenuity. If we were to associate his profiteering activities with any kind of capitalism, it would have to be the "adventurer's capitalism" that Weber identifies with the economically traditionalist[16] society. The picaroon's methods of enriching himself are, in Weber's terms, clearly not "rational"; it is the continual newness of adventure in his various profitable pursuits which attracts him.

In point of historical fact, this very spirit of economic adventurism played a rather important part in the growth of modern British capitalism, as Charles and Katherine George have recently pointed out in their closely documented study *The Protestant Mind of the English Reformation*.[17] Defoe's protagonist in this case turns out to be more Weberian than the complex historical phenomenon Weber was analyzing. For there is decidedly little spirit of adventure in the rogueries of Moll Flanders. Her variety of extralegal activities is not in the least a game

for her; on the contrary, she envisages virtually everything she does as a very serious business. The act of love
itself is no more than a piece of stock-in-trade for the
hard-working Puritan Moll; she certainly never gives the
faintest hint of any pleasure or emotional involvement in
connection with it. She views nearly all her activities as
means of making profit. One could hardly find a clearer
antithesis to the picaresque attitude toward money, its
significance, and its uses. In this respect, Moll is the most
duty-bound of Defoe's protagonists. Crusoe at least takes
a more perceptible measure of delight and satisfaction in
the management of his assorted home industries, and
there are some occasional glimmerings of a spirit of adventure or spontaneity in Colonel Jack, Captain Singleton, and
Roxana. But weighed against the model of picaresque
buoyancy, all the central figures of Defoe's fictions have
a leaden seriousness, and they move in a different sphere
of imaginative existence from that of the continental
picaro.

From the very outset of her career, money exercises an
uncontrollable fascination over Moll Flanders. In exchange for the first furtive caresses allowed to the older
brother of her foster family, she is given money, and it is
the money which immediately grips her imagination. "I
was more confounded with the money than I was before
with the love, and began to be so elevated that I scarce
knew the ground I stood on." And she can hardly with-
draw her attention from this mesmerizing acquisition. "As
for the gold, I spent whole hours in looking upon it; I
told the guineas over a thousand times a day." When Moll
finally takes her first lover it is the proposal of a hundred
guineas a year together with a first payment in advance
which overwhelms her. "My colour came and went, at the
sight of the purse and with the fire of his proposal together, so that I could not say a word, and he easily per-

ceived it; so putting the purse into my bosom, I made no
more resistance to him, but let him do just what he
pleased, and as often as he pleased." [18]

From this point on, Moll makes it very clear to her
readers that her principal motive in whatever she does is
profit. She measures people and their relationship to her
almost solely by the consideration of how much money
can be got out of them. "As for me, my business was his
money, and what I could make of him." "I had no spleen
at the saucy rogue, nor were his admissions anything to
me, since there was nothing to be got by him." Moll does
not even take credit for a temporary period of celibacy,
but freely admits that the lack of opportunity for profit
was the only reason for her virtue, as the attraction of
remuneration was all that could tempt that virtue. "I was
not wicked enough to come into the crime for the mere
vice of it, and I had no extraordinary offers that tempted
me with the main thing which I wanted." [19]

Whatever the dubious bypaths on which Moll sets her
shapely feet, she always keeps her eye fixed firmly on the
pound sterling. She is able to let the idea of profit over-
ride all moral considerations with such facility that one
may well wonder if the conscience of Defoe the moralist
has not been carried away by the imagination of Defoe
the lifelong entrepreneur. He has his protagonist report
one illicit venture in as glib a manner as this: "He stopped
the coach at a house where, it seems, he was acquainted,
and where they made no scruple to show us upstairs into
a room with a bed in it. At first I seemed to be unwilling
to go up, but after a few words I yielded to that too, being
willing to see the end of it, and in hopes to make something of it at last. As for the bed, etc., I was not much
concerned about that part." [20]

Whether it is a question of robbing a drunken gentleman with whom she has gone to bed or contracting a

legitimate marriage with a man who is the soul of probity, Moll's attitude is the same. The banker who helps her with her finances treats her with the greatest decency and frankness in every respect, but she sees him wholly in terms of how much profit he will bring. "I played with this lover as an angler with a trout . . . I made no scruple in my thoughts of quitting my honest citizen, whom I was not so much in love with as not to leave him for a richer." [21]

The moral universe of *Moll Flanders*, we find, is bare and depressingly cold. If the accumulation of money is the only important goal in human life, such things as love, friendship, the pleasures of the body and the mind, become highly suspect distractions, and one is forced to mistrust all other human beings as competitors and possible depredators. Ian Watt offers an interesting suggestion that the very flatness and sketchiness of psychology in the characters that surround Moll Flanders may reflect not a failure of imagination but an attempt at faithful representation of the effects on personal relationships of the criminal milieu. Watt probably gives too much credit to Defoe's art, but his sense of what has happened to human relations in Defoe's world is sound. We may add that the criminal milieu of the novel is in some important respects simply the capitalist milieu writ large, even if Defoe was not altogether conscious of the parallel. "Moll Flanders, and most of Defoe's other characters," Watt writes, "all belong on Crusoe's island; essentially solitary, they take a severely functional view of their fellows." [22]

One need not suppose, of course, that every capitalist lived in constant dread of betrayal by all whom he encountered. The whole idea of credit, so essential to the capitalist system, is based on the probity of the individual entrepreneur, that is, ultimately, on mutual trust. But relentless economic competition also quite naturally could

make men wary of one another, and here again Moll's
career represents the full realization of a possibility distinctly inherent in the capitalist situation. Her suspicion
toward her fellow men is nearly relentless. There are only
two people in her life to whom she becomes perceptibly
attached, and even to them she only partly opens herself.
The relationship between Moll and her governess is initiated entirely out of utilitarian motives, though a strong
mutual loyalty develops afterward between the two women.
The loyalty is strong, at least, on the part of the governess,
who goes to great pains to help Moll when she badly needs
help. The younger woman professes to her readers an
equal feeling of affection for the governess, but she is solely
a beneficiary in the relationship and does nothing on her
part to prove her affection. Genuine devotion to another
person would scarcely have been credible in Moll, and, in
keeping with her general character, she is careful to conceal from the old lady much of her private life and past.

The same is true in the anti-heroine's relationship with
her Lancastershire husband. The mutual revelation of the
two would-be deceivers—the scene which E. M. Forster
admires so much[23]—is a moment of real picaresque camara-
derie; but when the lovers soon after take leave of one
another, Moll makes certain to indicate that "still I reserved
the grand secret, and never broke my resolution, which was
not to let him ever know my true name, who I was, or
where to be found." [24] Even when the two come to America
together as man and wife, she does not let him in on the
zealously guarded secret of how much money she really
has.

In contrast to this ethos of suspicion which relates to the
predatory aspects of modern capitalism, the picaresque
capacity for openness and companionship retains connections with an older social and economic system. One of
the principal traits which distinguished traditionalist
societies from their capitalist successors was the strong

sense of community that pervaded the older kind of social organization.[25] A man did not regard himself wholly as an individual in the modern sense, that is, a distinct, separate, independent entity. He saw himself as part of a social organism. One can hardly suppose that there was no element of competitive struggle in the medieval local community, but more important was a deeply rooted feeling of mutual responsibility among the members of the community.[26]

When the picaresque novel first makes its appearance in sixteenth-century Spain, the cohesiveness of community of the medieval world is already in the process of disintegrating. The picaro determines to fend for himself partly because he is an individual who would not fit into the communal pattern in any case, but also because the weave of the pattern itself has begun to pull apart. Even so, he still preserves something of the traditionalist sense of mutual responsibility, the kind of responsibility developed in an organic community not only among individuals, but between trade or calling and the people it serves, and between one class and another. We have only to recall Lazarillo's disinterested loyalty to the indigent squire, or Gil Blas's virtually feudal devotion to Don Alphonse and his family.

Defoe's anti-heroine, on the other hand, has no real sense of responsibility toward other human beings or even toward herself, that is, toward the fulfillment of her own desires or the development of her own potentialities as a person. The only responsibility she does feel—and it is quite literally a responsibility for her—is toward the accumulation of wealth for its own sake. Weber's description of the practical philosophy of Benjamin Franklin could easily serve as a portrait of Moll and an explanation of her activities.

The peculiarity of the philosophy of avarice appears to be . . . above all the idea of a duty of the individual toward the increase of his capital, which is assumed as an end in itself.[27]

In fact, the *summum bonum* of this ethic, the earning of more and more money, combined with the strict avoidance of all spontaneous enjoyment of life, is above all completely devoid of any eudaemonistic, not to say hedonistic, admixture. It is thought of so purely as an end in itself that from the point of view of the happiness of, or utility to, the single individual, it appears entirely transcendental and absolutely irrational.[28]

Again, one may question whether such "worldly asceticism" was in fact the dominant spirit in the rise of capitalism, but Moll's long career as a thief is certainly characterized by precisely this kind of single-minded duty to the increase of capital. On rational grounds, it is not easy to explain her persistence in crime once she has amassed enough money to support herself comfortably for the rest of her days. After all, Moll gets no pleasure from the act of theft itself, except for a mild feeling of satisfaction at having achieved a special competence in a trade. The anti-heroine as a matter of fact is constantly terrified in her criminal activities over the risks involved; the thrill of danger has no appeal for her because she is a good bourgeoise who wants both security and an assured profit in her enterprises.[29] And she certainly does not increase her spending with the increase of her stock of money. Throughout her changes in fortune, she maintains the same standard of living: simple, never ostentatious, but always proper.

Moll's persistence in her career of crime offers an exact parallel to the familiar case of the businessman who cannot bring himself to retire from his business, even when he has made more money than he can use, because profit-making has become for him the only meaningful activity in life. And the various aspects of the thief's calling as described in *Moll Flanders* are consistently analogous to the daily business of a legitimate entrepreneur. Defoe's shoplifter and pickpocket repeatedly refers to her particular manner of acquiring wealth as "the trade." Like any trade, it must be managed with skill and, above all, with prudence. Like most lines of business, it has its on-seasons and off-seasons. "But the city was thin, and I thought our trade felt it a little, as well as other." After Moll's venture to Harwich, she learns that her business, like many others, is best carried out on a safe domestic basis without undue risks in a foreign market. "I was now returned to London, and though by the accident of the last adventure I got something considerable, yet I was not fond of any more country rambles, nor should I have ventured abroad again if I had carried the trade on to the end of my days." [30]

A sound instinct led Defoe, merchant and entrepreneur, to present thievery in terms of capitalist enterprise. We can go beyond the writer's own intention to observe that the effect of his representing the thief in this light is to expose some of the most essential—and most unattractive —traits of the capitalist. (John Gay, in fact, just six years after the appearance of *Moll Flanders,* was to make conscious satirical use of such a parallel between the respectable world and the underworld in *The Beggar's Opera.*) The acquisition of wealth, when the individual has no real responsibility to anything beyond acquisition itself, can quickly become an activity of pure depredation: the equation of capitalist and thief is not entirely an inappropriate one. Moll Flanders can have such an amazingly easy conscience about her crimes because, however much she professes the contrary, they are not really crimes for her. The only act that she could sense profoundly as criminal would be for her to shirk her duty to accumulate capital. We can listen to Moll playing lip service to the traditional morality she claims to accept, but she goes on immediately to the matters of finance which are her real concern. "We had £354 between us, but a worse gotten estate was scarce ever put together to begin the world with. Our greatest misfortune as to our stock was that it was all in money, which every one knows is an unprofitable cargo to be carried to the plantations." And nothing could illustrate more clearly how little guilt Moll really feels over her thefts than the moment when she makes a present of a watch stolen at a prayer meeting to her dear, rediscovered American son. Moll tenderly asks him to kiss the watch now and then for her sake, while she calmly observes, "I did not indeed tell him that I had stole it from a gentlewoman's side, at a meeting-house in London. That's by the way."[31]

Defoe's anti-heroine is made frequently to express her dismay over her life of sin and her apprehension of the divine judgment to which she must be called. There is little ground to doubt the honesty of Defoe's pious intentions, but it is clear also that his imaginative grasp of hell and damnation goes no further than the walls of Newgate prison. To be within these walls, amid "the hellish noise, the roaring, swearing, and clamour, the stench and nastiness, and all the dreadful afflicting things,"[32] is the most abject and pitiful state in which Defoe can imagine a human soul to be plunged. This is where the bankrupt—the damned of individualistic capitalism[33]—are sent to suffer for their mortal sin of insolvency. This is where thieves who have had the indiscretion to be caught—the underworld equivalent to bankruptcy among capitalists—are held till their final judgment is carried out. And this is where Defoe himself was committed for five dark months which he would never be able to forget. Nothing could be more hateful to the sturdy burgher than the complete descent from propriety that prison life forces on him: the bad odors and foul language, the dirt, the rags, the vermin. And nothing could be more maddening for the hardy entrepreneur than to be cut off by imprisonment from the possibility of regular profit-making.

It is not surprising that, since the hell of *Moll Flanders* lies no deeper than the foundation stones of Newgate, there is one universally efficacious golden bough with which a soul can descend into "all the horrors of that dismal place," and return unscathed. For the literalist Defoe, of course, the golden bough is literally gold and nothing else. As long as a man possesses an adequate supply of cash, he need fear no evil. "I knew that with money in the pocket, one is at home everywhere." (We might note the sharp contrast between this capitalist's aphorism and the picaresque attitude: the picaroon is at home everywhere with a portion of native wit in his head.) When Moll goes out shoplifting, she is in the habit of taking with her a substantial amount of coin of the realm as a kind of protective charm. Once, when she is nearly caught, the alderman who is called in to question her declares her absolute innocence as soon as he perceives the magic sign of gold in her pocket. The ultimate assurance that Moll's governess can give her in the despair of her imprisonment is to remind her, "Why, you have money, have you not?" [34] And once Moll is put on board ship as a convicted felon, the sight of her swollen purse immediately dazzles the crewmen and officers and transforms her state from prisoner for transportation to emigrating lady of quality.

This all-importance of money does not, however, make the concerns of Defoe's novel in any way petty. As Virginia Woolf has observed, quite the contrary is true. Because money—or the possibility of making money—is ultimately equated by Defoe's protagonists with life itself, it becomes for them something enormous, challenging, mysterious, perilous.[35]

One could find no better summary for the kind of significance money possesses in the world of *Moll Flanders* than these words of admonition which appear in a seventeenth-century capitalist tract entitled *The Worth of a Peny or a Caution to Keep Money.* "Whosoever wanteth money is ever subject to contempt and scorne in the world, let him be furnished with never so good gifts, either of

body or mind . . . In these times we may say with the wise
man: . . . better it is to die than be poore, for now money
is the worlds God . . . it gives birth, beauty, honour, and
credit . . . *Pecuniae omnia obediunt:* hence it is so admired
that millions venture both soules and bodies for the posses-
sion of it." [36]

If the characters in Defoe's novels never admit so frankly
that money is their god, money is certainly the one sure
sign for them that grace has been granted them by the
God of the Christians. Here, of course, it is appropriate to
recall Weber's discussion of the Puritan understanding of
worldly success and its positive spiritual implications.[37]
Moll Flanders is overwhelmed with gratefulness to Providence when her son surprises her with the news of a £100
a year income for her. Afterward, when Moll puts down
the £100 in silver before her husband, together with a
purse full of pistoles, he goes into the raptures of a prayer-
meeting epiphany. "Says my husband, 'So is Heaven's
goodness sure to work the same effects in all sensible minds,
where mercies touch the heart!' lifted up both hands, and
with an ecstasy of joy, 'What is God a-doing,' says he, 'for
such an ungrateful dog as I am!' " [38]

And it is true, at least in one sense, that *Moll Flanders*
is a fundamentally religious novel. If we adopt the broad
definition of religion suggested by the modern existentialist
theologians—an activity directed toward an ultimate concern—Moll can be described as a believer never remiss in
her religious duties. In this respect, Defoe's novel looks not
at all backward to the picaresque tradition, but forward to
the nineteenth century, to Balzac and the portrayal in the
novel of the all-consuming quest for wealth. Moll's literary
cousins are not Guzman and Gil Blas, but Félix Grandet
and Mr. Dombey. It is one of the essential characteristics
of the picaroon's nature not to get involved in religious
causes, whether the inner sanctum of the religion is in the

Vatican or at the Bourse. The picaroon really has no ultimate concerns. He lives from day to day, seeking the means
to fulfill his natural needs and desires from day to day. He
does not clench his will into a single-purposed effort that
comprehends every part of his life. There is a perceptible
relaxation of existential seriousness in the picaresque
novels: here, one feels, is life as it could be lived, with
difficulties to overcome, but without crushing responsibilities to bear. In the world of *Moll Flanders*, however,
the individual must carry the weight of a single unending
responsibility which necessarily converts the conduct of
his life into an austere discipline.

It would seem, then, more misleading than instructive
to call *Moll Flanders* a picaresque novel. It has one general,
coincidental similarity with the picaresque narratives—it
is the episodic fictional autobiography of a "roguish" figure
—but it derives from the English criminal biography, not
from the line of *Lazarillo;* and its sense of life, its imaginative atmosphere, and its moral feeling are in most significant respects antithetical to those of the picaresque novel.
The profound difference between Moll's single-minded
discipline and the distinctively picaresque mode of existence becomes strikingly clear when a quarter of a century
after the publication of Defoe's novel, the continental
picaro makes a full-dress appearance on English soil in the
person of Roderick Random.

CHAPTER FOUR

THE PICAROON AS
FORTUNE'S PLAYTHING

"IN SHORT, I HAVE TRAVELLED over the greatest part of Europe, as a beggar, pilgrim, priest, soldier, gamester, and quack; and felt the extremes of indigence and opulence, with the inclemency of weather in all its vicissitudes. I have learned that the characters of mankind are everywhere the same; that common sense and honesty bear an infinitely small proportion to folly and vice; and that life is at best a paltry province." [1]

At first glance, this is the sort of statement one might be tempted to seize upon as the proper epigraph for a book on the picaresque novel. These vigorous, incisive words—they are spoken by Cadwallader Crabtree, that angular caricature of Smollett's in *Peregrine Pickle*—seem to catch what is most essential in the career of a picaroon: the endless wanderings, the untiring assumption of new roles, the peaks and plunges of capricious fortune. Even the parallel structure of the two sentences reflects a fundamental characteristic of any good picaroon's peregrinations: "I have travelled . . . I have learned." And as a loyal member of the tribe of Lazarillo, Cadwallader has learned in particular to look at men with the eyes of a satirist, to see through the self-deceptions, the hypocrisy, the meanness of mankind. But the final, summarizing phrase of the Welshman's statement is not at all what we would expect to hear from a cousin germane to Gil Blas. These last words have the distinctive Smollett ring; they indicate the par-

ticular angle of vision of Smollett's picaresque world view
—"life is at best a paltry province." The more typical view,
of course, is quite the opposite: most picaroons see life
as a wide, rich realm that continually invites their exploration.

Among the prominent eighteenth-century novelists in
England, it was Tobias Smollett who most intentionally
and explicitly sought to place his narratives in the continental tradition of the picaresque novel. In the preface to
his first novel, *Roderick Random* (1748), Smollett affirms
his great admiration for Cervantes and for the Spanish and
French authors who practiced the method first conceived
by the creator of *Don Quixote*.[2] Now Don Quixote, like
Melville's whale, is one of those creatures of fiction that
comes to mean all things to all men, but Smollett makes
clear what is the chief innovation he thinks was made by
the history of the Knight of La Mancha. The appearance
of *Don Quixote* means for Smollett the advent of a new
realism in the narrative art, that is to say, the debunking
of romance, or rather, its conversion into a literary form
"more useful and entertaining, by making it assume the
sock, and point out the follies of ordinary life." [3] When
Smollett attempts a literal application of the *Don Quixote*
formula in his own *Sir Launcelot Greaves*, the intended
exposé of follies turns into a badly managed countryside
farce—which is romance assuming the sock with a vengeance. In the straightfoward picaresque narrative, however, without the anachronistic adornment of imagined
chivalry, Smollett is able to carry on the realistic impetus
which he senses in Cervantes and his successors.

If we keep in mind the necessary relativity of the term
realism, it is safe to say that the picaresque novel constitutes a realistic tradition in literature: it extends the scope
of the narrative form to embrace varieties of people and
places and activities which in the past were not ordinarily

considered proper subject matter. Smollett certainly shares in this picaresque thirst for reality. He tries to cram a great deal of "ordinary life" into his novels both as ordinary and as live as he can make it. The distinctive realism of *Roderick Random*, and the connection of this realism with the picaresque form of the book, is a question which it may prove profitable to explore.

The notion of realism in literature might be easier to talk about if it did not immediately involve a basic problem of epistemology. Founders of schools of literary realism have generally assumed that it is possible to call for the representation in fiction of *the* real world, but philosophy reminds us that we have no grounds for concluding absolutely that such a universal, objective reality exists, and if it does exist, we have no way of obtaining certain knowledge of it. We seem to share a more or less common set of given things "out there" among which and with which we live, but each of us looks at the data through the thickness, warp, coloring, and defects of his own pair of spectacles, and each of us consequently sees a world where at least some different elements are focused and blurred, magnified and distorted, illuminated and obscured. A reader of *Roderick Random* is likely to be struck by the fact that the twenty-six-year-old Scotsman who wrote it used a pair of glasses far more darkly tinted than the sort one would expect to find on the nose of a picaresque author. Smollett all his life remained enamored of picaresque tales, but we shall have to consider whether such a sullen, pessimistic view of the world as he seems to have held was really compatible with the picaresque form he adopted.

In the preface to *Roderick Random*, Smollett explains that he intends to imitate the model of *Gil Blas*, making allowances, of course, for the adaptation of the Hispano-French picaro to the distinctive aspects of British life. But apart from the changes necessitated by a different national climate, Smollett is not wholly satisfied with Lesage's work. *Gil Blas* is not "realistic" enough in the opinion of the Scottish would-be satirist for the simple reason that its world is too much pervaded by cheer and brightness. "The disgraces of Gil Blas are, for the most part, such as rather excite mirth than compassion: he himself laughs at them; and his transitions from distress to happiness, are so sudden, that neither the reader has time to pity him, nor himself to be acquainted with affliction. This conduct, in my opinion, not only deviates from probability, but prevents that generous indignation which ought to animate the reader against the sordid and vicious disposition of the world." [4]

Whether *Roderick Random* succeeds or not in inspiring its readers with indignation, the world it presents to them is certainly sordid and vicious, vicious not only in the sense Smollett meant—addicted to vice—but vicious also in the modern colloquial usage—fierce or savage. This should hardly surprise us in a picaresque novel. Though there may be considerable sunlight and insouciance along the picaresque way, Lazarillo's initial skull-rattling collision with the stone bull slammed home the lesson that no picaro could expect to be treated by his hard world with a gentle, loving touch. The battered pates and dislodged teeth, the chamber-pot ablutions and the breath-odors of emetic virtue, the merciless verbal clubbings and the brutal practical jokes, are very much part of the picaresque set of conventions from its beginnings in Spain.

Such rough and often unpleasant elements are first of all the traditional properties of a crude, slapstick stage comedy, and the picaresque novel puts them to much the same comic use as the theater. But the novel, in contrast to stage comedy, is by nature a descriptive literary form. It cannot often get away with using what is rough or scatological merely as a dramatic property; it is usually drawn by the inner logic of its own narrative form to *portray* its comic "properties," and, what is more important, to portray the social milieu to which they belong and from which they derive. The picaresque novels send their protagonists traipsing down all sorts of twisting, garbage-strewn by-ways that have in general been considered off-limits for the more respectable heroes of traditional narratives. The attention that they give, then, to the coarser aspects of existence, is not only a comic convention, but also a genuine extension of the frontiers of realism for fiction.

And there is every indication that Smollett's portrayal— like Hogarth's—of physical as well as moral sordidness, was in large part the representation of a very real side of life in eighteenth-century England which was often neglected by the more genteel forms of literature. The poised rhythms of the heroic couplets—interrupted only occasionally by the rougher cadences of a Swift—may tend to make one forget the most unheroic belly noises of the lower orders of English society in the age of neoclassicism. But the picaroon's business in life is to wander up and down all the social strata, hearing all sounds, seeing all sights, smelling all odors. Before we condemn Smollett's concern with filth as simply excessive or obsessive, let us see how a recent historian of the period describes the general appearance of an eighteenth-century town in England.

The first noticeable thing about these towns would have been the stench. There was no sanitary system; an open cess-pool in the court often served the richer inhabitants; the poor, as with Eastern peoples today, made a public convenience of every nook and cranny . . . The houses of the poor were one or two room hovels made only of weatherboard with a pitched roof placed back to back; or they were the houses of the rich, deserted because their owners were seeking more salubrious suburbs—ramshackle warrens of filth, squalor, and disease.[5]

And if we are inclined to conclude too quickly that the

savagery of existence reflected in *Roderick Random* is merely the product of Smollett's peculiar temperament, we might recall the same historian's concise description of eighteenth-century England as a fertile ground for the seeds of ecstatic Methodism. "There was an edge to life in the eighteenth century which is hard for us to recapture. In every class there is the same taut neurotic quality—the fantastic gambling and drinking, the riots, brutality and violence, and everywhere and always a constant sense of death." [6]

Precisely this sort of sharp "edge to life" is captured in the works of Smollett as it is almost nowhere else in the fiction of the period. It would seem, then, that at least some of the fierce or menacing aspects of the world of *Roderick Random* are justifiable on the same grounds that Smollet himself would have justified them: the desire to present ordinary life as it is.

But one can hardly get past the opening chapter of Smollett's novel without sensing that reality shows here a kind of ugly face which could not be explained solely on the basis of the brutality of any brutal age. In a recent article, Ronald Paulson has tried to explain these unpleasant elements in Smollett precisely in terms of a disparity between the picaresque, novelistic form and Smollett's desire to write rigorous satire. Paulson sees *Roderick Random* as a Juvenalian satire with Roderick as the satirist's persona, observing vices (not participating in them), and scourging the vicious. According to this analysis, the persona and the vices become objectionable because they have been set in the more fully concretized reality of a novel, instead of a satirical poem. In any case, we are asked to regard *Roderick Random* less as a conventional picaresque novel than as a selection of congenial elements from the picaresque tradition for use in a Juvenalian satiric anatomy.[7]

Paulson's discussion is suggestive, and it does demonstrate that Smollett's involvement with the tradition of Roman satire in some ways modifies the picaresque form as he handles it. But I believe that *Roderick Random* is more directly in the line of the continental picaresque novels than Paulson would allow. To begin with, it is clear that Smollett, in looking across the Channel at Lesage, did not distinguish, as Paulson does, between satire and picaresque; and, indeed, unless one extends the picaresque novel to include all criminal fiction, satire is implicit in the picaresque situation. Roderick's partial detachment from his surroundings—as the case of Gil Blas suggests—is characteristically picaresque, and is in itself no indication that the protagonist is being used as a Juvenalian persona. The brutality with which the world treats Roderick, and with which he occasionally pays back his enemies, does not have to be explained in terms of satiric "scourging," for such elements, as we noted earlier, are present in the picaresque novel from its beginnings. But the conception of *Roderick Random* as formal satire runs into real difficulties in trying to see the violence in the novel as part of a thematically unified, coherent satiric design. The trouble is that the violence is often too harsh for any imaginable satiric purpose and it is too generalized: it pervades the novel and never seems fully under the author's control.

Young Roderick's surroundings are not merely cruel, like the ordinary picaresque environment, or like a society under the Juvenalian scourge, but are shot through with lurid tinges of real sadism. Characteristically, Roderick's schoolmaster, in order to prevent the orphaned youth from making progress in his studies, hits upon the following ingenious expedient: "On pretence that I had writ impertinent letters to my grandfather, he caused a board to be made with five holes in it, through which he thrust the fingers and thumb of my right hand, and fastened it with whipcord to my wrist, in such a manner as effectually debarred me the use of my pen." [8] The cruelty practiced by the people whom Roderick encounters is often not merely the product of callousness but stems from a delight in cruelty, even a pleasure in inventing refinements of cruelty. The most frightening moments on board the *Thunder* are representative of the general moral ambience in which Roderick must swim and struggle not to sink. It is enough to recall the "cure" that Captain Oakum and Dr. Mackshane undertake for sixty-one critically ill men by forcing them all back to their posts. "On the whole, the number of the sick was reduced to less than a dozen; and the authors of this reduction . . . applaud[ed] themselves for the services they had done to their king and country." [9] This kind of savagery reaches nightmare intensity when Smollett describes his hero chained hand and foot to the deck, unable to move or even turn, while in the thick of a heavy cannonade, he is splattered with the dashed out brains of one marine and the torn up entrails of another.[10]

From the beginning of his story, Roderick reports to his readers a kind of life which is not simply harsh or rugged, but where the whole world seems to have joined hands in a monstrous conspiracy against him. The catalogue of persecutions that Smollett's hero presents as the account of his boyhood is the pattern of his later career as well:

> I was often inhumanly scourged for crimes I did not commit; because, having the character of a vagabond in the village, every piece of mischief, whose author lay unknown, was charged upon me. I have been found guilty of robbing orchards I never entered, of killing cats I never hurted, or stealing gingerbread I never touched, and of abusing old women I never saw . . . I was once flogged for having narrowly escaped drowning, by the sinking of a ferry-boat in which I was pas-

senger; another time for having recovered of a bruise occasioned by a horse and cart running over me; a third time for being bit by a baker's dog.[11]

The enumeration of calamities in this passage indicates one possible psychological ground for the sadistic element which is so ubiquitous in the world of *Roderick Random*. Smollett's hero, we see, is both victimized by the community and on his own account inveterately accident-prone. The need to victimize someone may itself stem from a rage of frustration in the face of calamity. The protagonist of the novel, of course, could not be permitted the luxury of giving vent very often to such rage; by the conventional assumption alone which underlies Smollett's narrative, the hero must remain ultimately virtuous—though there are moments in the novel when Smollett comes close to losing sight of this ideal—and even kindly disposed toward his fellow creatures. But it would appear that in the sort of society in which Roderick lives, the frequency of frustrating mishaps is at a maximum—which is to say, over against a widely held social ideal of order, there exists a reality of social disorder. Society does not have the means, for example, to assure the safety of travel, the security of property, the general inviolability of the individual. Consequently, daily experience in such a society can build up a high pressure of frustration in its members which may demand an explosive outlet. The typical social background for the picaresque novel is a world where the old social order is disintegrating but is still regarded as though it were continuing undisturbed. It is not surprising, then, that violence—occasionally even sadistic violence—is a pattern of behavior congenial to the picaresque world. Smollett's novel, in any case, makes such violence peculiarly central to the picaroon's experience.

When Roderick and Strap arrive in London for the first time, the loyal barber makes an observation on the treatment afforded them by the metropolis much to the same effect as Roderick's description of his boyhood. "God send us well out of this place; we have not been in London eight-and-forty hours, and I believe we have met with eight-and-forty thousand misfortunes.—We have been jeered, reproached, buffeted, pissed upon, and at last stripped of our money; and I suppose by and by we shall be stripped of our skins." [12]

There is a significant difference between this encounter of the country boy with the big city and the usual introduction of the small-town picaro to urban wiles. London does more than shake some of the innocence out of the head of Smollett's hero; it knocks him down hard, and when he is down, it kicks him, and when he gets up, it trips him and starts the whole procedure over again. As Roderick progresses in his adventures—until the last volume when Smollett begins to rain *dei ex machina* down through the air—we are impressed with a growing sense of the ubiquity and relentlessness of the conspiracy mankind has shaped against this well-meaning individual.

"One night about twelve o'clock, as I returned from visiting a patient at Chelsea, I received a blow on my head from an unseen hand, that stretched me senseless on the ground; and was left for dead, with three stabs of a sword in my body." In this case it is a cowardly rival of Roderick's who is settling an account of resentment against him by the use of hired assassins, but this experience is the archetypal experience of Roderick's world. The young Scotsman is, in rapid sequence, attacked in the streets, accused of theft, seized and wounded by a press gang, subjected to the brutalities of a tyrannical ship's captain, and then nearly drowned by his crewmates in a shipwreck. Making his way to shore, he fights a duel with his most sadistic tormentor from the ship, is struck down from behind as he is about to win the duel, is stripped of all his valuables and clothes and abandoned on the beach. Half-dead with fatigue and cold and beating, he crawls to the nearest peasant's cottage, from which he is "tumbled out like a heap of dung" [13] and passed on from door to door among the villagers—the minister's house included—because no one is humane enough to take the trouble of caring for a dying man. There is no end, it would seem, to the villainy of mankind in the world of *Roderick Random*.

And yet the account of Roderick's adversities and adventures is not altogether the story of a Gulliver in the land of the Yahoos. If Smollett's novel were only this, it would not really qualify as a picaresque novel. For perhaps the most basic assumption underlying the picaresque world view is the conviction that while life is hard, life is also good. Experience is a positive thing—the picaroon is constantly seeking more of it. Humanity itself, despite all its knaveries and hypocrisies, remains decent at the core. Without this supposition that man is basically decent, or at least that some men are decent, the picaresque virtues of compassion and companionship would be totally inexplicable. And Roderick Random, for all the resentment he harbors against a brutal and inimical world, continues to believe that life is good and that it is worth preserving. His natural sympathy for human beings in misery is never stifled, as he demonstrates, for example, in his willingness to share his last farthing with a diseased and abandoned prostitute. "Such extremity of distress must have awaked the most obdurate heart to sympathy and compassion." [14] Though his world swarms with scoundrels and tyrants, there are also sound, lovable human beings with whom Roderick can enjoy the warmth of mutual affection—his nautical uncle, Tom Bowling; Mr. Morgan, the spunky Welsh ship's surgeon; Mrs. Sagely, the kindhearted old lady who finally takes in the picaroon after the shipwreck; and (despite the feudal subservience of his relationship to Roderick) the faithful barber, servant, and companion, Strap.

"'A light heart and a thin pair of breeches goes through the world, brave boys, as the song goes, eh!'"[15] This is the counsel that old Tom Bowling gives to the future picaroon. And although Smollett's hero may sometimes follow the advice with clamped teeth and clenched fists—in contrast to the spontaneous carefreeness of a Gil Blas—he follows it nevertheless. It is part of the picaresque convention that experience should never substantially alter the given character of the hero, and this means that even a picaroon in Smollett's world must maintain a certain distance from the world so that it will not impinge too much upon him or distort the contours of his particular personal integrity.

I had endured hardships, 't is true; my whole life had been a series of such; and when I looked forward, the prospect was not much bettered; but then they were become habitual to me, and consequently I could bear them with less difficulty. If one scheme of life should not succeed, I could have recourse to another, and so to a third, veering about to a thousand different shifts, according to the emergencies of my fate, without forfeiting the dignity of my character beyond a power of retrieving it, or subjecting myself wholly to the caprice and barbarity of the world.[16]

A major indication of the distance that exists between Roderick and his world—a distance that allows both for the preservation of personal integrity and for comedy—is his habit of seeing human beings in terms of caricature. We must consider, of course, that it is first Smollett the author, and not his protagonist, who is taking advantage in his novelistic method of a special genius for caricature. But this sort of genius is one which is particularly congenial to the situation of the picaresque hero. It insists on representing the thing itself entirely through external appearances, and is quite what we would expect in a view of the world "from the road." On the road, a man may look over his fellow's features as he strides by him, but he has neither the time nor the repose to enter into anyone else's inner life; moreover, in such swift scrutiny, it is understandable that some features will be magnified and others overlooked.

The method of the caricaturist in presenting reality has a paradoxical effect. On the one hand, the artist, through the sheer boldness of exaggeration of his strokes, can create the impression of an unusual intensity of life in his creatures. The element of distortion in caricature, on the other hand, leaves us with the feeling that it is perhaps more than real, and therefore not quite real, that it exists in its own peculiar sphere of fantasy.[17] This sense of the not-quite-real is often the feeling we get about Roderick's world from the descriptions he gives us of it. As a result, what might be discomposing or even threatening frequently proves to be wonderfully absurd. Humanity is completely dehumanized by Smollett's quick pen. The people his protagonist encounters are viewed as baboons, grasshoppers, spiders; their cheeks are alforjas, their teeth fangs, their jaws nutcrackers, their noses hooked paring knives. There is nothing sinister, however, about this humanity "disguised, and transfigured and transmographied" (the words are Mr. Morgan's) into dumb brutes and inanimate objects. The striking characteristic of Smollett's dehumanization of people is the exhilarating play of unrestrained imagination—as in the delightful description of the fury of M. Lavement over his wife's infidelity: "With one blow, he split the mortar into a thousand pieces, and, grinning like the head of a bass viol, exclaimed, 'Ah, traîtresse!' " [18]

It cannot be denied that there are moments of boisterous good fun in Roderick Random. Roderick himself, though there is little of exuberance or buoyancy in his personality, is a fellow who, when the occasion offers, takes manly pleasure in draining a bottle, tumbling a wench, rousing the watch, or what have you. Are we to conclude, then, that there is an underlying contradiction between the comic or fun-loving elements implicit in the novel's picaresque form, and the stubbornly morose view of humanity which Smollett passed on to his hero? It is well to remember that lightheartedness is not the only significant picaresque trait. The picaroon's life is characterized by delight in experience, on the one hand, and by adversity on the other. Correspondingly, insouciance is one pole of the picaroon's psychological field, but resentment, or at least a deliberate posture of tough-mindedness, is the other pole. The main concentration of energy of a picaresque personality may be near one pole or the other. Smollett's protagonist offers a rare instance in which the attraction is clearly far stronger to the pole of resentment.

But before we get too encumbered with gravitational fields and electric apparatus, perhaps we ought to consider plainly what is the precise location in existence of the picaresque hero. The picaroon, before all else, is an outsider. Granted, he is an outsider who can make and keep friends, and in this respect he remains distinct from the tortured and isolated outsiders of twentieth-century fiction, but the way he chooses is nevertheless a devious and personal way, not the straight, clearly marked, foot-worn path of society at large. It would be a rather pretentious exaggeration to describe the picaroon as an individual "in quest of a personal truth," but one can safely say that the anti-hero does instinctively reject the stale and inapplicable truths accepted by the generality of men, even if he sets up no higher goal for himself than to get along well in the world. By remaining apart from the stability of the fixed social order, he takes upon himself both more freedom and more vulnerability than the ordinary, socially "adjusted" man. Rugged individualist that he must be, the picaroon has to assume direct and personal responsibility for shaping the course of his existence, and in this regard he is freer than other men. But because he is divorced from the kinds of security that society offers its members in good standing—the assurance of an accepted belief[19] that allows one to know which values are important and which are not—the outsider may sometimes feel less, not greater, control over his destiny than other men feel.

In its classic philosophic formulation, the problem raised by the picaroon's peculiar marginal location is the conflict between free will and determinism. The novel, of course, does not abstract the two contradictory positions, but presents them in terms of the individual's immediate apprehension of the world: the hero, in his daily experience, can either sense himself to be the master of his destiny, or he can feel that he is an object buffeted about by fortune. In the former case he is likely to be imbued with a sense of power and even exhilaration, in the latter case he will be moved by resentment or stoic resolution or perhaps both. The picaroon as master of his fate is the picaro, jack-of-all-trades, skilled manipulator, adept deceiver, artist of disguises, adaptable to all situations and all men. The picaroon as the butt of fortune is the man of many adversities, continually tossed on the breakers of a sea of vicissitude, never allowed rest or security.

It is interesting to note that these two alternative stances which the anti-hero can take are counterparts of the two alternatives of heroism open to the traditional hero. Heroism involves an assertion of will; the great man extends himself to do a deed which is beyond the reach of the little man. But heroic achievement can take place either through action or through passion. In the latter case, the act of heroism is the hero's ability to assume a burden of suffering others could not carry. Neither kind of heroism, however, can exist outside a context of absolute solidarity between the hero and his society. The active hero realizes in his achievements a set of ideals which he holds in common with the other members of his society, and his achievements are generally for the sake of the others as well as for his own glory. The suffering hero—the ritual scapegoat—voluntarily becomes a victim because the complete devotion he feels for his fellow men makes him willing to suffer for their sake. It is easy enough to see what happens when the organic connection between the hero and his society is seriously impaired. The active hero has no one but himself to benefit in performing his actions: he becomes the picaro, master opportunist.[20] The suffering hero, on the other hand, discovers that his suffering is meaningless because he has nobody for whom to suffer. Instead of being a ritual victim, he finds himself merely the victim of fate—a fate that seems arbitrary and indifferent to him. Instead of being a scapegoat, he is merely a scapegrace—both a ne'er-do-well and literally "one who escapes grace."

Smollett's own life shared something of the marginal position of his picaresque heroes. As a Scotsman in London, he remained in certain respects a permanent outsider, and he was disposed to see in himself a creature cast out into an alien and unsympathetic world. Smollett in fact had the misfortune later in his career to become the most hated kind of outsider—the foreigner who appears to the natives to have insinuated himself into the ruling circle. Hired by the generally despised Lord Bute, favorite of George III, to defend his "Scottish" ministry, Smollett, by advocating the unpopular administration in *The Briton*, won only scorn and resentment for himself and his fellow Scotsmen.

It is probable, then, that this sense of undeserved hurt—as well as the love for tales of adventure—was what attracted Smollett to the picaresque novel. Indeed, if Americo Castro is correct in his conjecture that the author of *Lazarillo* was a Jew,[21] then the whole picaresque vision of life was first shaped by an outsider, and it is certainly

not surprising that a figure like Smollett would find congenial elements in such a vision. In a letter to David
Garrick dated April 5, 1761, Smollett expressed his own
awareness of the human condition in the following terms:
"I am old enough to have seen and observed that we are
all playthings of fortune and that it depends upon something as insignificant and precarious as the tossing up of a
halfpenny, whether a man rise to affluence and honours, or
continue to his dying day struggling with the difficulties
and disgraces of life." [22]

And in the parody of the traditional prophecy of the
hero's birth with which Smollett begins *The Adventures
of Roderick Random*, his future picaroon is presented quite
literally as a plaything—a tennis ball knocked out of sight
by a furious blow from the devil. Smollett happily chooses
to describe his hero as the sort of plaything meant to hold
up under a great deal of rough use, a plaything, in fact,
that is employed in particular because of its resilience.
Roderick manages to bounce back no matter how stinging
the blows from fortune are, but he is unable to exert much
more control over his fate than the tennis ball tumbling
through air exerts over the racket swinging to meet it. The
correlation between this sense of helplessness and the feeling of being an outsider has already been suggested. If you
do not play along with the people who set up the rules, you
are likely to find that your life clashes with the rules, that
the rules, the rule-makers, the whole world around you,
grind on with relentless indifference or even enmity toward
you and your individual integrity.

A paradigm of this general predicament is offered in
the clash between Roderick and Mackshane related in
Chapter XXX. Roderick is accused of espionage; his diary
written in Greek characters is brought forth in evidence
as a book of ciphers. The young surgeon's mate insists
that all he did was to inscribe the most innocent personal

observations in ordinary Greek letters. Mackshane, seconded by the captain, damns Random for a scoundrel, asserting that he knows real Greek when he sees it as well as any man. And then, to prove his accomplishments as a classicist, he emits a burst of rough-sounding dialect, which Roderick recognizes as Gaelic. When two "Greek-speaking" sailors are summoned as witnesses, one of the pair turns out to be Irish, and he answers Mackshane in Gaelic, stoutly affirming it to be as authentically Greek as the pillars of the Parthenon.

The ship's complete isolation from the world—which in effect makes the ship itself a microcosm—underscores the maddening aspect of Roderick's position as an outsider. He knows what the truth is. Unfortunately, in the world where he finds himself he alone knows what the truth is. He has no doubts about what is Greek and what is not, but there is no way he can prove he is right, there is no just authority to whom he can appeal. It is for this reason that he feels himself the helpless victim of powers he cannot influence. If the entire ship's complement were to insist that white were black and black white, Roderick would have no means to avoid the dire consequences of maintaining the opposite, while his sense of integrity would prevent him from merely assenting to the lie. When Smollett conceives the circumstances of his picaroon in such terms, it is hardly surprising that the vision of life conjured up by the novel is of an immense and insidious conspiracy. It is not the best of all possible picaresque worlds, but it is one kind of world which it is decidedly possible to derive from the basic picaresque situation.

There remains one peculiar feature of *Roderick Random* that deserves consideration. We noted earlier that many picaresque writers feel constrained to tag onto their novels a post-picaresque coda in which they can get the

hero settled down happily and comfortably. But what is
both surprising and frustrating for a reader of Smollett's
novel is the discovery that nearly the entire last third of
this long book moves into a most unpicaresque world.
Smollett, as his many admirers have attested, is one of
the great masters of the rapid-paced, rough-and-tumble
narrative, but throughout the relation of Roderick's romance with Narcissa, the writing is so comically bad that
it offers an object lesson in what can happen to a picaresque writer when he leaves familiar ground. Smollett,
unfortunately, was not quick to learn the lesson: within
five years, he would publish *Ferdinand Count Fathom;*
his attempt in the second half of that novel to convert
the narration of a rogue's adventures into a romantic tale
produces as disastrous a failure of imagination as any
novelist of stature has ever been guilty of. More significant
for our purposes, however, the last part of *Roderick Random* illustrates by way of contrast to the earlier sections
of the novel several elements that are egregiously incon-
genial to the picaresque spirit.

Romance, to begin with, is not a picaresque forte. The
movement of the picaroon is always toward a variety and
abundance of experience, and he is not very adaptable to
the single focus of an all-consuming passion. On the technical level, the picaroon does not ordinarily possess
enough inner life to enable the author to involve him con-
vincingly in a great love. The later chapters of *Roderick
Random* make it painfully evident that Smollett flound-
ered with this difficulty. He clearly is not capable of con-
veying an authentic sense of the experience of love, and
he tries to hide his inadequacy in a turgid flood of ex-
clamatory rhetoric. "Good Heaven! what were the thrill-
ings of my soul at that instant! my reflection was overwhelmed with a torrent of agitation! my heart throbbed
with surprising violence! a sudden mist overspread my

eyes! my ears were invaded with a dreadful sound! I paused for want of breath, and, in short, was for some moments entranced." [23]

As a substitute for the representation of an inner world which is beyond him, Smollett makes his protagonist go through the wildest and most exaggerated outward gestures in order to convince us of the profound emotions he is experiencing. Precisely because physiology is Smollett's only correlative for inner experience, he can be effective in representing feelings like anger, pain, embarrassment —giving beatings or being beaten or being made a fool of—while he fails completely in describing love. The technique of representation is exactly the same, but the object has changed, and that makes all the difference.[24] This is the way we are supposed to know that Roderick is suffering from jealousy: "It set all my passions in a ferment, I swore horrible oaths without meaning or application, I foamed at the mouth, kicked the chairs about the room, and played abundance of mad pranks that frightened my friend almost out of his senses. At length my transport subsided, I became melancholy, and wept insensibly." [25]

The fair object of all this thrashing-about has even less convincing reality than Roderick's passion for her. Sporadically, he conjures her up as a kind of Guinevere or Virgin Mary to inspire him in his travails. This is a particularly ironic reversal on Smollett's part, when we recall that the picaro is by origin a deliberately deidealized verson of the knight errant. "I fell asleep," Roderick tells us of a night in France far away from his beloved, "and my fancy was blessed with the image of the dear Narcissa, who seemed to smile upon my passion, and offer her hand as a reward for all my toils." [26] Smollett, master of the bold and vivid caricature, is at a loss to describe Narcissa. Instead of trying to represent her appearance, he bedecks her with garlands of noble abstractions—meekness, innocence, beauty, and the like—or, alternately, he draws over her a diaphanous veil tremulous with erotic excitement.

The novelist himself, moreover, seems to sense some uneasiness as to whether he really has got anywhere with the entire romantic episode. More than once he has Roderick confess despair over his inability to put into words the presumably unequaled extremity of his passion. "I am tempted to commit my paper to the flames, and to renounce my pen forever, because its most ardent and lucky expression so poorly describes the emotions of my soul." [27]

Walking into the last section of *Roderick Random* is like stepping from a sea beach into a hothouse. We leave the harsh but bracing salt air of the picaresque world to enter into the rhetoric-perfumed, tear-watered sphere of the novel of sentiment. The noble feelings that move the characters in these chapters are typically accompanied by tears: picaroon Roderick himself and even old Tom Bowling yield to the general melting mood. Erich Auerbach has caught the distinctive tinge of this kind of sensibility in his discussion of the Abbé Prévost. "In the literature of the eighteenth century tears begin to assume an importance which they had not previously possessed as an independent motif. Their effectiveness in the border region between the soul and the senses is exploited and found to be especially suited to produce the then fashionable thrill of mingled sentiment and eroticism." [28]

The sentimental passages in *Roderick Random* seem particularly strained and incongruous after what has preceded them because the picaresque novel is fundamentally an antisentimental mode of representing reality. The cult of sensibility places premium value on feelings in themselves; emotions are sought after, savored in the experience, treasured in memory. But the picaresque hero is oriented toward action, not feeling. In his rough world, he has neither the leisure nor the interest to relish the nuances and the degrees of purity of his own emotions.

Sentimentalism,[29] moreover, assumes that certain kinds of emotions should immediately and necessarily be attached to certain relationships. This is the source of the annoying call for stock responses that characterizes sentimental literature. A father should inspire filial piety in a son; a fair maiden, respect and devotion in a young man; an orphan, pity and charity in the hearts of all, and so forth. Sentimentalism, in short, is an aprioristic mode of response to the world. It presupposes that certain kinds of relationships among human beings have a fixed and universal moral value. Sentimentalism is in this way a self-appointed protector of traditional values and traditional relationships. The picaroon, however, learns to take very little for granted. He may not consciously reject traditional values, but he is essentially an empiricist. He bases his actions and his estimate of people upon what experience teaches him. No relationship is a priori sacrosanct for the picaroon, and nothing could be more out of place in him than the expectation of a stock response from his readers.

The decline from the picaresque of Roderick Random foreshadows what was soon to occur on a wide scale in European literature. Born in the flowering of the Renaissance, the picaresque novel is the characteristic expression of a vigorously active individualism in a rugged, competitive world. But as the age moved toward sentiment in the latter half of the eighteenth century, before long it would be only the dissident spirit who could feel at home in the picaresque tradition of hardship and adventure.

CHAPTER FIVE

THE PICAROON DOMESTICATED

ᮌᮩᮞ ᮌᮩᮞ ᮌᮩᮞ

THE YEAR 1748 was an eventful one for the young English novel. In February, Smollett's *Roderick Random* made its appearance. By December, all seven volumes of Richardson's *Clarissa* were out at the bookstalls. And before the end of the year, Fielding had finished *Tom Jones* and was waiting for the final volumes to come off the presses early in 1749. It is hardly surprising that the reading public of the time should be struck by the dramatic contrast between Fielding and Richardson in temperament, method, and purpose. Critics ever since have taken pains to trace the pattern of antitheses presented by the two great eighteenth-century novelists.[1] But at the same time there was a marked tendency among readers of the period to lump Smollett and Fielding together. It was widely believed, in fact, when the anonymous first edition of *Roderick Random* was offered to the public, that Fielding was the author. Smollett on his part, in characteristic fashion, far from thinking he wrote too much like Fielding, accused Fielding of writing too much like him: he denounced Fielding's Partridge as a blatant plagiarism of his own Hugh Strap.

The superficial points of contact between the two writers are abundant enough, and it is natural that a man as thin-skinned as Smollett should find even surface contact abrasive. But the author of *Roderick Random* had little cause for real worry. Even if Fielding had taken anything from him—and considering the dates of composition for *Tom Jones*, this seems highly unlikely—the English writer's aims and methods were so different from the Scotsman's that anything borrowed would have had to undergo a radical transformation.

At first glance, both *Tom Jones* and *Roderick Random* seem to follow the same general picaresque plan. A passionate but honorable young man is unjustly banished from the family estate. He takes to the road, where he is soon joined by a Sancho-like companion (in both cases, a Latin-quoting barber). In his role of vagabond, the hero wanders through all sorts of low life and, eventually, high life as well. We follow him on the familiar picaresque passage in and out of the clutches of thieving innkeepers, the arms of wanton females, the grip of prison doors. His often-professed devotion to his beloved does not deflect him from a career of adventure, for his story is oriented toward action, and neither he nor the characters that people his world possess any real quality of innerness. The hero's way leads from country to city, from relative rural simplicity to the sphere of refined corruption. In the end he emerges unscathed to marry his heart's choice, receive his withheld patrimony, and return to the country to settle down on the land of his ancestors.

But if the two figures seem to be cut after the same pattern, it is clear that Roderick and Tom are fellows of very different cloth. What distinguishes them, moreover, is not merely a matter of individual characterization: Tom Jones exists in a completely different world from that of Smollett's picaroon. It is a picaresque world only in a deliberately limited fashion. For in Fielding's great novel the picaresque tradition merges with—or rather, is assimilated by—a way of apprehending and reporting reality quite distinct from the mode of narrative first developed in the Spanish novels of roguery. The precise nature of this process of assimilation will become clear if we consider closely a passage from one of the characteristically "picaresque" episodes of *Tom Jones*.

It is both the nature and the fate of the picaroon forever to be involving himself in scrapes, and Fielding's protagonist is no exception to this rule. In the third chapter of Book IX, Tom, after rescuing the amiable and underclad Mrs. Waters from her would-be assassin, forces an entrance to the inn at Upton with his very obviously female companion. The landlady naturally takes umbrage at the intrusion of such an indecent pair, and she issues forth with upraised broom in defense of the propriety of her household. This is the way Fielding relates the reception Tom gets from the Upton landlady:

Our travellers had happened to take up their residence at a house of exceeding good repute, whither Irish ladies of strict virtue, and many northern lasses of the same predicament, were accustomed to resort in their way to Bath. The landlady, therefore, would by no means have admitted any conversation of a disreputable kind to pass under her roof. Indeed, so foul and contagious are all such proceedings, that they contaminate the very innocent scenes where they are committed, and give the name of a bad house, or a house of ill repute, to all where they are suffered to be carried on.

Not that I would intimate that such strict chastity as was preserved in the temple of Vesta can possibly be maintained at a public inn. My good landlady did not hope for such a blessing, nor would any of the ladies I have spoken of, or indeed any others of the most rigid note, have expected or insisted on any such thing. But to exclude all vulgar concubinage, and to drive all whores in rags from within the walls, is within the power of every one. This my landlady very strictly adhered to, and this her virtuous guests, who did not travel in rags, would very reasonably have expected of her.

Now it required no very blamable degree of suspicion to imagine that Mr. Jones and his ragged companion had certain purposes in their intention, which, though tolerated in some Christian countries, connived at in others, and practiced in all, are however as expressly forbidden as murder, or any other horrid vice, by that religion which is universally believed in those countries. The landlady, therefore, had no sooner received an intimation of the entrance of the above-said persons than she began to meditate the most expeditious means for their expulsion. In order to this, she had provided herself with a long and deadly instrument, with which, in times of peace, the chambermaid was wont to demolish the labours of the industrious spider. In vulgar phrase, she had taken up the broomstick, and was just about to sally from the kitchen, when Jones accosted her with a demand of a gown and other vestments to cover the half-naked woman upstairs.[2]

There are times when it may be profitable for criticism to begin with the obvious, and the most obvious difference between this passage and traditional picaresque narrative is the fact that Fielding does not use his hero as a first-person narrator. The difference is, of course, a technical one, but as is usually the case in literature, the technical organization of the work relates directly to its substance. Histories of literature generally explain the first-person form of the picaresque novel as a simple and, in many cases, primitive means of imposing some kind of unity on a series of episodes: we know that all the various adventures belong together in one continuous story because they all have happened to the same individual rogue who tells us about them. If the first-person narrator is merely a unifying device, *Tom Jones*, with its nonepisodic, masterfully interlinked plot, certainly needs nothing of the sort. But, in any case, it is difficult even to imagine that Fielding would let Tom tell his own story; for, beyond the consideration of technical unity, the picaresque use of the autobiographical form implies a world view totally alien to the great English novelist.

The grammatical subject "I" that precedes all the other words in the text of most picaresque novels is also a philosophical subject "I" which has precedence over all the

objects it encounters. As we discovered in our consideration of *Lazarillo,* this does not necessarily imply an ethos of
relentless egoism. But it does mean that in the order of
certainties, the "I" comes first. The picaro, or, to view the
question genetically, the picaresque author, finds himself
in a world where the center cannot hold—which is precisely why the picaroon is an inveterate vagabond, turning and turning in a widening gyre. The world is usually
deceptive, often inimical, never trustworthy. The picaroon
can, however, be certain that his own unprotected skin
will suffer if it is exposed to the inclemency of sun, rain,
cold, or a vigorous fist, and that his own stomach will
ache if he fails to get something inside it; so he directs
his attention first to dealing with these hard facts of
reality.

The picaresque novel affirms the primacy of individual
experience—to begin with, the most basic aspects of individual experience—in a kind of existence where any
larger order must be very much in question. It is a literary
form characteristic of a period of disintegration, both
social disintegration and the disintegration of belief. Like
Descartes, the picaresque writer finds any existing systems
to be of the shakiest kind, and he, too, tries to effect a
basic reconstruction by beginning again with the one self-
evident fact of the experiencing "I." [3] Chance rules in the
picaresque world: the individual cannot really understand
his world or control it. All he can depend upon is his own
pliant resourcefulness with which he must learn to make
the best of chance as it comes along.

Now one of the important effects of seeing Tom Jones's
adventures always through the translucent medium of
Fielding's controlling intelligence is effectively to eliminate any element of chance from the narrative. The author
of *Tom Jones* refers again and again to Fortune, to whose
whim the lamentable protagonist is presumed to be total-

ly subjected, but it becomes increasingly apparent that when Fielding says Fortune he means Fielding. Like his great Victorian disciple, Thackeray, Fielding makes us continually aware that he holds the strings and that he will make his puppets hop about exactly as he pleases until he chooses to set them down. But the metaphor does not quite do justice to Fielding. While he is constantly finding ways to affirm his authorial mastery over his characters, he wants his readers to understand that it is not a completely arbitrary mastery. For Fielding's art belongs more to neoclassicism than it does to Renaissance "low" realism; he is in many ways closer to Pope than to Smollett or Defoe. And he begins with the key assumption of neoclassicism that reality presents an intelligible structure, that events occur in an order of cause and effect perceptible to the intellect and capable of logical analysis.

Let us try for a moment to imagine how a writer like Smollett in the mainstream of the picaresque tradition might have reported the piece of action that Fielding deals with in the three paragraphs quoted above. Smollett's first-person narrator, using a prose decorous but always swift-paced in pursuit of rapid action, might have described this moment of the episode in the following fashion: "Incensed by the intrusion of such a scandalous pair as we must have seemed to be, the landlady seized a broom from the corner and, brandishing it like a war club, made straightway for me." It may be instructive to consider why Fielding felt he needed some four hundred words to convey this simple piece of information to his readers. In terms of the content of these three paragraphs, all but the conclusion is a satiric excursus, containing a variety of comments on morals and inns and innkeepers. Yet it is remarkable that the passage makes itself felt neither as desultory in its own progress nor as extraneous to the progress of the story. On the contrary, it bears the hallmark of Fielding's distinctively neoclassical prose: each piece is linked carefully and firmly to the next, like the chain rings of mail armor. Fielding may write at large, but never at random.

On careful examination, our passage proves to be a neatly reasoned progression, moving from step to step while the relationship of each successive step to what has gone before is meticulously indicated by the appropriate transitional phrase. Every sentence—with the exception of the last, which is merely a translation of the sentence before it—constitutes a new moment in the argument, following clearly from the preceding moment. The sequence (transitional phrases are indicated in parentheses) runs as follows: 1. *initial assertion*—the inn is a reputable one; 2. *consequence*—undesirables are excluded ("The landlady therefore . . ."); 3. *explanation of consequence through formal generalization*—bad doings invariably give inns bad names ("Indeed . . ."); 4. *qualification*—no inn can be absolutely chaste ("Not that I would intimate . . ."); 5. *specific application of preceding generalization*—the innkeeper in question does not expect absolute chastity ("My landlady . . ."); 6. *qualification of 4*—some kinds of promiscuity can be excluded ("But . . ."); 7. *specific application of qualification*—the landlady in question would exclude vulgar promiscuity ("This my landlady . . . this her virtuous guests . . ."); 8. *relation of facts of narrative to the preceding argument*—the appearance of Jones and Mrs. Waters could easily suggest that their intentions fall under the category of vulgar promiscuity ("Now . . ."); 9. *consequence of 1–7 followed by 8*—the landlady seeks to expel Jones and his companion ("The landlady, therefore . . ."); 10. *implementation of 9*—the landlady seizes a broom ("In order to this . . .").

Now it is in just this sort of subject matter of domestic farce that the picaresque element of chance or coincidence ordinarily makes itself most felt. For farce depends to a great extent on the unexpected, and sometimes improbable, conjunction or collision of two or more incongruous elements—the face and the pie, the fashionably shod foot and the banana peel, the hairy-legged suitor and the petticoats of Charley's aunt. One might well expect to encounter in a picaresque novel an intersection of occurrences which would result in a farcical situation of the kind we have: the hero happens to join company with a female who, for reasons having nothing to do with him, is embarrassingly underclad; he then stumbles into the path of a most irascible and suspicious landlady who immediately misconstrues the admittedly compromising appearances; several other personages successively happen to appear on the scene, from which concurrence of parties ensues a wild free-for-all replete with bloodied noses, cracked pates, and, presuming one relishes this sort of thing, Homeric laughter. Fielding, however, has imposed even on his farcical scenes a clearly indicated pattern of cause and effect. Or to look at the question from the other end, he sees at all times in the events of reality a definite logical order.

The picaresque novel usually catches hold of the world by its individual and particular handle. After being cheated by half-a-dozen innkeepers, the picaroon may make some tacit generalization about bewaring of innkeepers, but his mind does not really operate on the plane of generality. He will not often be interested in formulating the generalization,[4] hardly ever in undertaking an analysis of the general question. Fielding, on the other hand, is constantly moving back and forth between particular and general, and in this respect he is more closely related to the English essayists of the period than to the tradition of the novel. Because reality presents to him a logical order, the particular can always be subsumed under a general category, and the particular can be used to inquire into the general, or vice versa. Thus from the Upton landlady and her reputable house, Fielding can move out to inns at large, to the question of reputation and morals, and even to the general prevalence of promiscuity in the presumably Christian countries. Human existence, in other words, is governed by certain general laws which are accessible to the writer who has applied himself to a long and careful course of study in both the word and the world. It becomes clear why it is so important for Fielding to write his novel in his own person, from an authorial vantage point, very much master of all he surveys.

In this connection, the strict dignity of diction that Fielding preserves throughout his writing is indicative of the stance toward his subject that he has adopted. Smollett's language is also decorous, as we have noted, but not elegant and majestically expansive as Fielding's is: the author of *Tom Jones* goes to deliberate excesses in order to emphasize the contrast between the decorousness of his language and the decided indecorousness of the subject matter. So Tom's sudden irruption by main force into the Upton hostelry, in the company of a half-naked woman, is referred to as "taking up residence." Fornication is "conversation of a disreputable kind" or "foul and contagious proceedings." When the landlady "receives an intimation" of the arrival of the objectionable guests, she does not think how she can throw them out most quickly, but rather she begins to "meditate the most expeditious means for their expulsion."

At this point, Fielding moves into mock-heroic diction: his bellicose landlady is said to have "provided herself with a long and deadly instrument, with which, in times of peace, the chambermaid was wont to demolish the labours of the industrious spider." Like Pope's designation of a pair of household scissors as a "deadly engine," Fielding's use of language appropriate to heroic warfare has the effect of underscoring the unheroic aspects of the subject at hand. But Pope's employment of such epithets works two ways, for in the sexual *double-entendre* of his poem, that "glittering forfex" does indeed make itself felt as a deadly weapon. Fielding, on the other hand, is quick to collapse the structure of serious battle language which he has begun to build. "In vulgar phrase, she had taken up the broomstick." He is reminding us who the landlady is, who he is, and, by implication, who we, his readers, are. The force of "in vulgar phrase" is exactly the opposite of Moll Flanders' use of "in plain English." When Moll employs the latter formula, it is a signal of impatience, of a desire to sweep away any highfalutin talk that may have preceded. Fielding's phrase, by contrast, is concessive: well, if you must, then it was a broomstick the good lady seized. While describing a lively comic episode in an English country inn, he makes us aware of his authorial elevation over the "low" reality in which his story takes place.

The traditional picaresque novel, by virtue of its first-person form, immerses us directly into the low milieu that is the picaroon's native habitat. Indeed, the picaresque novel makes no distinction between high and low spheres of reality; the rich-veined marble of ducal palaces is neither more nor less interesting and appropriate as the setting for the roguish activities of a Gil Blas than the grease-and-smoke-stained panels of a country inn. If, as I have suggested, the picaresque novel is an expression of the sink-or-swim individualism characteristic of a period of social disintegration, it is quite understandable that it should present reality to us in a way that ignores social distinctions—or, rather, ignores the implications of such distinctions concerning a hierarchy of subject matter for

literature. Fielding accepted the affirmation of the picaresque tradition that all social strata and sectors were
equally valid material for the narrative art, and particularly
for the narrative of satirical intent. He was, moreover, too
broad-minded and generous-spirited a man to look on the
plebeian milieu in which he set his characters with anything like superciliousness or disdain. In comparison, however, with the typical picaresque novel, the low reality
presented in Fielding's books is viewed *de haut en bas*.
Unlike the narrating picaroon, our omniscient author has
his feet on firm social ground in cultured and respectable
territory, and it is only by choice that he directs his attention to the more vulgar precincts.

And what we have said of the narrator holds true for his
protagonist as well. Though it may be "the universal
opinion of all Mr. Allworthy's family that he [Jones] was
born to be hanged," [5] Fielding never really lets us doubt
that he has a far better destiny in mind for his hero. Tom
is a picaroon on a string, and a golden string, at that. His
creator may let him dangle in the sink of contemporary
life—either social (Molly Seagrim) or moral (Lady Bellas-
ton)—but we sense all along that Tom does not actually
belong in these lower regions and that he will at last be
pulled up out of them. In sharp distinction to *Roderick
Random,* Fielding's novel keeps constantly before its readers the possibility of the return home and the rehabilitation
of the wanderer: Partridge, forever mulling over his hare-
brained scheme to bring Tom back to Allworthy, is a
principal instrument in keeping the prospect of return
alive. And unlike most picaroons, Tom has all along in
Squire Allworthy someone to whom he would want to return. In this respect, *Tom Jones,* a novel with such
conscious epic overtones, is closer to the Homeric narrative
and its noble wanderer than to the picaresque tales and
their vagabond scamps: Tom, like Odysseus (and like

Joseph Andrews) is sent out on a journey in order that he may ultimately return home.

But in any case, Fielding's protagonist is by no stretch of the imagination a rogue. His passionate nature or his imprudence involve him in some questionable sexual adventures, but he remains through it all a young man of impeccable moral principles. "Though I have been a very wild young fellow," he tells his army lieutenant as he warms to the moralizing mood which seizes him now and then, "in my most serious moments, and at the bottom, I am really a Christian." [6] It is only people who judge by the extraneous that condemn Tom as a good-for-nothing vagabond bastard. The more discerning individuals he encounters on his travels somehow are all struck immediately by the fact that he is a gentleman, whatever the appearances may be. And Tom is, in fact, no less than an admirable young country gentleman on a picaro's itinerary. The journey is not a way of life for him, but a kind of penance that he is made to undertake for the sins of his youth, both actually and only apparently committed. The reader, however, can have little doubt that the young gentleman will somehow eventually be restored to his proper sphere.

It is clear, both from the prefatory material in *Tom Jones* and from the characterization of the protagonist, that Fielding had a definite moral purpose in mind in creating the figure of Tom. The relationship between this moralist's conception of character and the typical conception of character in the picaresque novel is not quite antithetical, but it is certainly problematic. The picaroon, we should remember, is not wholly an amoral figure, even in his most roguish embodiments. He affirms through his adventures at least one significant moral value: the courage of self-reliance, of human ingenuity, in an arduous existence that allows the individual no other resources.

To a limited degree, *Tom Jones* dramatizes a similar

value. Tom must be thrown out on his own in order for the story to take place—and also in order for the moral purpose of the story to be accomplished. Though Tom plainly does not possess the slightest particle of roguish ingenuity, he shares with the picaroon an unshakeable persistence and a singular resilience in the face of adversity. In order for Tom to practice these virtues, it is necessary that he be expelled from the Eden of the Allworthy estate into a world that has at least something of the picaresque quality of harshness about it. "The world, as Milton phrases it, lay all before him; and Jones, no more than Adam, had any man to whom he might resort for comfort or assistance." [7] But there are no flaming swords to bar irrevocably the return to this paradise, and outside its gates is no stony wilderness but a bright English countryside where a benign providence will walk at the hero's elbow, or at least close enough to toss him a shilling or two when needed. Tom may be thrown on his own, but, unlike the picaroon, he is never wholly on his own. He does not have to struggle to survive, and, certainly, the struggle for survival is not a motive force in the narrative, as it is in the traditional picaresque novel.

Ultimately, there can be no serious doubt about the safety or well-being of Fielding's hero because Fielding means him to be a model of virtue—however imprudent—who must eventually receive his Just Deserts. The happy ending is not a conventional afterthought, as it often seems to be in the picaresque novel, but the entelechy toward which the entire plot is directed: virtue must be rewarded, iniquity reproved, and each individual set in the place assigned to him by his birth and by his inherent moral worth. Fielding states clearly in the dedication of *Tom Jones* that the purpose of his novel is "to recommend goodness and innocence," and he goes on to sketch a conception of the novel as an extended moral *exemplum* "in which virtue becomes, as it were, an object of sight, and strikes us with an idea of loveliness, which Plato asserts there is in her naked charms." [8]

It is not easy to reconcile this moralistic program for the novel with some of the memorable comic creations of *Tom Jones*—Squire Western and his sister, Partridge, Honour, even Bridget Allworthy. An abundance of imaginative energy has been expended upon those figures which could hardly be justified in terms of moral purpose alone. Squire Western is a great character in English fiction not because he offers an apt satire on the pigheaded narrowness of English country squires in the eighteenth century. Rather, Fielding has discovered in the mannerisms which comprise the blustering Squire a way of producing distinctive and convincing life; and like all good novelists, he regards with paternal joy the life he has produced as something precious in and of itself. But the moral formula of the dedication seems to be more directly responsible for the existence of such good or bad characters as Allworthy, Blifil (the neatly antithetic contrast to Tom), Thwackum and Square, Attorney Dowling, Mrs. Miller, and most important, Tom Jones himself.

But after all, one might object, Tom is notoriously a red-blooded hero, and hardly the sort of character to have been invented merely to serve as a pattern of virtue. We should keep in mind that the tradition which sees in Tom one of the great daring portraits of a real man in the English novel is fostered by Thackeray, and such a prude *malgré lui* was likely to be overly impressed by Fielding's willingness to admit freely the existence of sexual instincts in his hero. It is true that the author of *Tom Jones* presents us a deliberately deidealized and consequently "realistic" image of a hero. Like the picaresque writers, he sees both his hero and all mankind as members of an animal species, impelled and limited by many of the drives and necessities

common to all animals. But however "wild" Tom may
claim to be, one gets the feeling that his weakness of the
flesh is not much more than a redeeming fault which prevents him from becoming the oppressive prig that models
of virtue—witness Grandison—seem inevitably to become.
The benevolent and righteous young man who vehemently
denounces his own "vice and folly" is certainly no blood
cousin to the pleasure-loving adventurer and opportunist
of the novels of roguery.

Up to this point, all the connections considered between
Tom Jones and the picaresque tradition have proved to be
in matters of externals, and one may well wonder if there
is anything more essentially picaresque in a novel that,
from most points of view, is so characteristically neoclassical. The two terms are not mutually exclusive, but the
neoclassical feeling for rational order and stability in art
and in life is very different from the picaresque vision of
a haphazard and spontaneous existence unfettered by
social bonds. Now Fielding is especially a faithful heir to
the great Augustans in envisaging his role as a writer
fundamentally as the job—one might say, responsibility—
of a satirist. But satire, of course, is also one of the most
essential properties of the picaresque novel from Lazarillo
onward. We have seen in connection with *Gil Blas* how
the picaroon's marginal position in society allows him to be
a keen and unprejudiced observer of human foibles and
hypocrisies.

There is, however, another aspect of the picaresque
situation, apart from the angle of vision of the picaroon
himself, which invites the exercise of satire. The anti-hero
is an outcast, and because he remains at the center of our
field of attention and sympathy, his very existence raises
some question as to how clean are the hands that have
done the casting out. He is a rogue, but he is quite frank
about his roguery, while among the respectable citizens

of the world he lives in, the leering face of real vice hides under a mask of hypocrisy. Because he is an outsider, it is very easy for the insiders to condemn him while congratulating themselves on their own moral superiority, and were he not so quick in jumping out of the way, they would also be glad of the opportunity to trample him underfoot. The picaroon, therefore, becomes a kind of touchstone for the virtue of other men; when he comes in contact with them, their own moral genuineness is frequently put to the test.

The virtues of the picaresque hero, as we noted earlier, are principally the virtues of the heart. One of the reasons why he never even puts up a pretense of moral punctiliousness is that he is not concerned in the least with theories of morals. His own ethical behavior—for better or for worse—is the result of natural instinct, just as his desire for wine, women, and what have you is the result of natural instinct. One must assume, of course, a certain fund of decency in human nature in order to arrive at any such "naturally" moral man, but this is precisely what the picaresque writer assumes, however keenly aware he is of the corruption that exists on all levels of society. The picaroon has in some respects an immunity to moral contamination because he is committed to remain faithful to his own healthy instincts, to his own natural self. There are times when this commitment to be honest with himself is just what makes the picaroon a target for general censure; these are the times when the ostensible rogue serves most effectively as an instrument to expose the moral unsoundness of others.

The sort of ethic presented by this whole positive aspect of the picaresque code is one which is strikingly congenial to Fielding's way of thinking. Tom Jones is moral in just the way that the picaroon is moral: in his fidelity to his own conscience, even when his acts lack the appearance of virtue in the eyes of the respectable world. Tom, in proper picaresque fashion, works largely on intuition in questions of morals; Fielding means him to stand in sharp contrast to such moral theoreticians as Thwackum and Square. When the philosopher-pedagogue Square is caught behind the curtain in Molly Seagrim's bedroom, he thoroughly deserves our censure as well as our laughter because he has espoused a moral theory which excludes all such license; therefore it is only as a hypocrite that he could allow himself the pleasure of Molly's company. Tom, on the other hand, is no theoretician. He follows his physical instincts with Molly as directly and frankly as later on he will follow his instincts of benevolence with the indigent Mr. Anderson. Because of this naturalness and honesty, we sense nothing mean or lascivious in Tom's sexual activities, just as we feel no real turpitude in the thieving activities of most picaroons. The picaresque hero usually manages to preserve a fundamental soundness even in his illicit practices, and, consequently, when he is denounced by "proper" society, he is likely to reflect upon it a high satiric light which will illumine its deepest moral flaws.

The author of *Tom Jones,* then, in creating a hero who is no more than a gallows bird in the eyes of those who consider themselves his betters, has adopted the fundamental satiric situation of the picaresque novel. As far as Fielding's satirical purposes are concerned, people in the novel mistreat Tom in order to expose themselves; they judge him that they may be judged by us. One brief example should indicate how the process works. In Book XII, Chapter VI, Partridge, in one of his frequent moments of more than generous candor, confides to the assembled company at an inn his solemn conviction that his master is a hopeless lunatic. Having heard this assertion, Partridge's listeners comment in turn on the suspected Jones.

As each speaks, his own pretentiousness and his own particular kind of narrow self-centeredness shine through every sentence. The kind of comedy at work is the traditional humor of professions and self-interest, but it is significant that a quasi-picaresque figure is used here to trigger the familiar satirical sequence.

The puppet-show man immediately coincided. "I own," said he, "the gentleman surprised me very much when he talked so absurdly about puppet-shows. It is, indeed, hardly to be conceived that any man in his senses should be so much mistaken; what you say now accounts very well for his monstrous notions. Poor gentleman! I am heartily concerned for him; indeed he hath a strange wildness about his eyes, which I took notice of before, though I did not mention it."

The landlord agreed with this last assertion, and likewise claimed the sagacity of having observed it. "And certainly," added he, "it must be so; for no one but a madman would have thought of leaving so good a house to ramble about the country at that time of night." [9]

In the much-quoted preface to *Joseph Andrews*, Fielding makes clear that the vices he sees as the proper target of a comic writer are those which spring from affectation—namely, vanity and hypocrisy.[10] So for him, as for Molière, the basic satiric movement is the act of unmasking. The picaroon, by his very location and status, is both an unmasker and an instrument to induce men to unmask; and in regard to the latter function, Fielding's foundling is very much a picaroon and *Tom Jones* a picaresque satirical novel. With this important difference: always above Tom, the inadvertent unmasker, is the author deftly separating layers of appearance from the reality they disguise with the fine-edged instruments of his irony.

The favorite object of picaresque satire, we recall, is the whole range of vices that wraps itself in the cloak of respectability. Fielding's satire as well is aimed largely at the so-called respectable world. This is why he follows the picaresque example of using an ostensibly improper figure as his hero, and this is why authorial irony is so important in his general strategy. For the basic trick of irony is to avow something while actually undermining it and suggesting that the opposite is in fact true.[11] Irony, consequently, is ideally suited to unmasking pretensions or hypocrisies by claiming—just a little too vehemently—to accept them at face value.

The passage we considered earlier offers a fine example of Fielding's use of irony to indicate a distinction between the appearance and the reality of virtue. In contrast to his ironic treatment of such manifestly satirical characters as Square, Thwackum, and Blifil, the technique here is relatively subtle. What these three paragraphs do in effect is to develop progressively an ironic definition of the term virtue. At the outset, we are told that the inn is "a house of exceeding good repute" frequented by "Irish ladies of strict virtue." Virtue, the juxtaposition informs us, concerns itself with reputation, and there is at least a suggestion—which will be further developed—that virtue consists in reputation. Moreover, the one word of excessive emphasis (an important signal of irony), "strict," makes us begin to suspect that the ladies may be concerned more with a virtuous appearance than with virtue itself. Fellow guests of the strictly virtuous Irish ladies are Scotswomen "of the same predicament." "Predicament," originally a scholastic logical term, is a decorous, Latinate way of saying "state of being," but in the eighteenth century as now, it was commonly used to imply an undesirable or distressing state of being.[12] Virtue, we infer, when not considered merely as a matter of reputation, is a state from which females seek to extricate themselves, and in which perhaps they may be forced to remain because they lack the natural charms necessary for the extrication.

Fielding now appears to condemn all illicit pleasures,

speaking with righteous indignation on behalf of the landlady and her very proper lady guests. Again, the perceptible note of excessiveness in his statement of condemnation
suggests that these virtuous ladies do protest too much.
"So foul and contagious are all such proceedings, that they
contaminate the very innocent scenes where they are committed." The pathetic fallacy of "innocent scenes" is the
key here to the ironic exaggeration: we are apparently
called upon to pity the poor scene which is infected by
such corrupt goings-on. The remainder of the sentence,
however, indicates what the real concern of these virtuous
parties is: "contamination" is a matter of reputation, of
giving "the *name* of a bad house, or a house of ill *repute*"
to an inn.

The act of unmasking which was begun in the first paragraph is effectually completed by the major qualification
of the second paragraph. Fielding, who is accustomed to
shift nimbly from one ironic posture to another, uses the
excessive emphasis of irony in two new ways here. In the
preceding paragraph, overemphasis was employed to cancel out what was ostensibly asserted (the dedication to
chastity of the traveling ladies) by suggesting that the
opposite might be true. In the first part of the second
paragraph, the exaggerated stress is used to cancel out
what is ostensibly being asserted (the ladies' willingness
not to insist on absolute chastity) by suggesting that it,
and, alas, much more, is true. Vestal virginity, Fielding
informs us, is not within the reach of a country inn. The
landlady would not hope for it, "nor would any of the
ladies I have spoken of, or indeed any others of the most
rigid note, have expected or insisted on any such thing."
The emphasis of denial makes itself felt at every point: in
the introduction of a third group ("or indeed any others"),
in the triple stress on "any of the ladies," "any others,"
"any such thing," and in the doubling of the verb ("ex-

pected or insisted"). The inference we are led to draw is that the ladies of rigid note would be most distressed if the inn they stayed at offered nothing but vestal prospects to them.

Such is the stuff that "virtue" is made of—provided, of course, that the blemishes of the natural material can be completely covered by the veneer of respectable appearance which is, after all, the essence of virtue. Developing this idea, Fielding uses ironic stress in the next two sentences by way of exclusion, to suggest that what the ladies are concerned about is not virtue at all but mere propriety in the most limited sense of the word. "But to exclude all vulgar concubinage, and to drive all whores in rags from the walls, is within the power of every one." Emphasis is achieved here through the parallel structure and through the rhetorical flourish that puts the two infinitive phrases in initial position. But on what does the emphasis fall?—on "all *vulgar* concubinage," "all whores *in rags*." The stress on these words implies that it is this, and only this to which the virtuous ladies object. They are not averse to the pleasures of the night, as long as they can be well hidden, but the ladies will rise up in wrath against harlotry that has the face to parade in public, bedraggled and besmirched.

This reading is reinforced by the one superfluous clause that Fielding introduces into the next, and final, sentence of the paragraph: "This her virtuous guests, who did not travel in rags, would . . . have expected of her." We hardly needed to be told that the good ladies from the North and the West did not travel in rags. Again the emphasis has the effect of exclusion: *all* that can be asserted about the ladies in contrasting them to the "whores in rags" of the previous sentences is the fact that the ladies do not travel in rags. By now, we have been prepared to make the inference that the epithet "virtuous" is attached to the ladies chiefly because they do not travel in rags, and that, in the last analysis, this is all virtue means for such people.

In the third paragraph of our passage, Fielding returns to the narration of action, but as he does, he deftly sums up the distinction he has been making between the profession and performance of virtue and sets it in a larger cultural perspective. That activity which Jones and Mrs. Waters appear to be contemplating but in fact are not (at least not yet Jones), and which the virtuous ladies would appear to condemn but in fact long to enjoy, is "tolerated in some Christian countries, connived at in others, and practiced in all" although it is "as expressly forbidden as murder, or any other horrid vice, by that religion which is universally believed in those countries." Fielding's irony, in one last sweep, completes its task of undercutting the particular kind of hypocrisy it has been attacking through the passage. Weakness of the flesh, Fielding suggests, is a universal human frailty: it is certainly one for which he himself would show the most generous understanding. But the commonly professed morality of the Christian countries places the yielding to this weakness on the same level with the most heinous of sins. The official morality, it is clear, is likely to be used more frequently as a club for the self-righteous to swing than as a measuring stick for Everyman to stand against. All such contrasts between lip service and real belief, between pretending to live by a morality and living by it, are suggested in the deliberately glib and ironic exaggeration of Fielding's characterization of Christianity as "that religion which is universally believed in those countries."

The passage we have been considering amply illustrates Fielding's exercise of authorial irony as an instrument for unmasking affectation, and it is understandable enough why such a writer would be attracted to the anti-heroic hero of the picaresque novel, who, by his ambiguous status among men, is also an unmasker of them. And yet Fielding's irony itself indicates the fundamental difference between him and the picaresque novelists, and it forces us to the conclusion that *Tom Jones* is not a picaresque novel, but a novel where important picaresque elements have been assimilated by a different tradition.

Let us recall for a moment what is implied in the ordinary picaresque application of irony. Conscious irony always involves the exercise of intellect with the particular effect of establishing a superiority for the ironist over the object of his irony. But the picaroon's irony is employed in a completely different context from Fielding's, and both the significance of intellect and the kind of superiority established are very different. The picaroon lives in an unsure world, and from one point of view his fondness for the stance of irony is not unlike that of a person who feels unsure in a social situation and adopts irony to assert his own importance and—as we observed in the case of Gil Blas—to create a kind of invulnerability for himself. Everything that floats into range is a potential target for the picaroon's irony. His irony need not have any positive moral purpose; it is critical without necessarily assuming a clear standard of desired behavior. Ultimately, picaresque irony is an individualist, asocial exercise of the intellect, and as such it reflects the condition of rootlessness which is the heart of the picaresque situation.

Fielding's ironic treatment of virtue, on the other hand, should indicate what is true of all his irony: that he knows very much where he stands and wants to make it quite plain to his readers where they should stand. His ironic critique of hypocritical prudery presupposes a positive standard of behavior that the hypocrites fail to live up to; this is a kind of irony that never forgets its social responsibilities. The social implications of Fielding's irony could hardly be better described than they are by A. R. Humphreys in his illuminating essay "Fielding's Irony: Its Methods and Effects": "His irony, far from being radically disturbing like that of Swift, is, in intention, corrective and orthodox; it undermines deviations from a healthy, sensible, social morality; it prunes society of perversions. Unlike the irony of Gibbon or Samuel Butler II, it does not unsettle traditional ethics and Christian orthodoxy—it is the irony of integration rather than disintegration." [13]

Although by the time Fielding wrote his masterpiece, English letters had largely lost the Augustan feeling for stability and lucidity, *Tom Jones* is a thoroughly Augustan novel. The world as seen in its pages is solid and certain; every man has his place in a stable social order; there is a clear-cut, common-sense Christian morality as a guide for action. Concomitantly, order is the keynote for the narrative as well; the novel must be constantly under the perfect control of the author who continually envisages the unity of all the complex parts.

Fielding's use of the picaresque novel in *Tom Jones* represents a characteristically neoclassical enterprise of transformation. The neoclassicist, unable himself to write the heroic epics he admired so much, took pride and pleasure in a skillful and decorous adaptation of presumably alien genres to the epic. Reynolds, in the sixth of his *Discourses on Art*, clearly expresses this general neoclassical interest in the sublimation of low material: what Reynolds recommends to his audience of painters is precisely what Fielding has consciously set out to do with the picaresque novel in the "comic epic" form of *Tom Jones*. "Very finished artists in the inferior branches of the art, will contribute to furnish the mind and give hints, of which a skilful painter, who is sensible of what he wants, and is in no danger of being infected by vicious models, will know how to avail himself. He will pick up from dunghills what by a nyce chemistry, passing through his own mind, shall be converted into pure gold." [14]

The case of *Tom Jones* is instructive because it suggests the point at which the picaresque novel had arrived and what would be happening to it in the future. The picaresque novel was the product of a certain moment in history—which is a shorthand way of saying that without the concurrence of a certain stage in development of literary traditions, certain social conditions, a certain prevailing sense of life, and the specific creative genius that produced *Lazarillo*, the picaresque novel could not have come into being. Of course, once somebody had gone ahead and written a picaresque novel, there was one major condition less to be fulfilled, and a whole flock of such novels could be written; but it is also clear that the other prerequisite conditions would eventually cease to exist, so that it would some day be at least improbable for anyone to write a picaresque novel pure and simple. There also may be some truth in Ortega y Gasset's suggestion that a genre can be worked out like a quarry,[15] but one weakness of that metaphor is that it considers the genre in and of itself, apart from the various historical conditions external to it which are necessary for the flourishing of the genre.

The state of society, the struggle for existence, the world at large, looked appreciably different to the eyes of an intelligent observer in 1750 than they would have looked in 1550. And in terms of literary development, by mid-eighteenth century, new techniques of fiction were becoming available which made it increasingly difficult for a writer to restrict himself to the literary aims and methods implied in the work of a sixteenth-century Spaniard. The time of the picaresque novel as a living genre was passing. But the picaresque vision would remain to fructify imaginations and to help inspire new worlds of fiction. And the situations and methods of the picaresque novel had become part of the general stock of the novelist. Writers would continue to attempt what Fielding had done so skillfully in *Tom Jones:* to take important elements from the picaresque novel and to reshape them for new uses in new surroundings.

CHAPTER SIX

HEIRS OF THE TRADITION

꧁ꕥ꧂   ꧁ꕥ꧂   ꧁ꕥ꧂

DURING THE nineteenth and twentieth centuries, the novel has pursued a career of growing complexity and diversity which at times has bewildered readers and critics as well. There are few definitions of the novel that do not snap at some point when they are stretched to fit all the various works of fiction generally referred to as novels. Perhaps criticism ultimately may be forced to something in the nature of what Northrop Frye undertakes in his suggestive though sometimes questionable work on theory of genres.[1] Mr. Frye feels that it is misleading to speak of "the novel" in the broad way we are accustomed to do. He sets up a general category of "prose fiction," within which he distinguishes four significant forms: the novel, the romance, the confession, and the anatomy. Prose fiction offers pure examples of the four forms and, more commonly, a wide variety of combinations and permutations involving two or more of the forms.

There may be some doubt whether criticism is justified in so contravening established usage as to exclude from the realm of the novel books everyone thinks of as novels. But the appeal of such a division as Mr. Frye suggests bears witness to the perplexing diversity of the genre. One begins to suspect that this stubborn resistance to categorization is itself the most crucial generic characteristic of the novel. André Gide in fact has distinguished the novel as the one genre which is essentially "lawless." Most great novels, Gide asserts, follow their own internal rules or principles of structure; the original novelist generally seems to take the law into his own hands.[2] It is worthy of note that with all the many faces and various colors that the novel has shown to the world during the last century and a half, an impressive number of novels continue to organize their characters and their worlds in something akin to the picaresque situation. The relationship with the picaresque tradition is often indirect, and sometimes perhaps unintentional, but it makes itself felt with a surprising degree of frequency.

Or perhaps it is not so surprising. For what, after all, are the most essential characteristics of the picaroon? He is a man who does not belong, a man on the move, and a man who takes things into his own hands. The picaresque novel, then, is born out of the conflict between the individual and his society. Social conditions in England, France, America, and elsewhere during the nineteenth and twentieth centuries have made such conflict increasingly likely. By the nineteenth century, the cash nexus was widely felt to have replaced more traditional bonds between men. In this new, mobile society, a thinking person born in the middle or lower classes had more grounds to question his inferior position because so many of those above him on the social ladder were there not because they "belonged" but simply because they had amassed more capital than he. The new industrialized, bourgeois society, moreover, promulgated a standard of mediocrity and crass materialism that was likely to embitter or estrange the sensitive individual.

These negative aspects of modern bourgeois culture continue to make themselves felt in the twentieth century, and they have been compounded and complicated by the unchecked expansion of bureaucracies and by the development of methods of control and "motivation" of the populace which, whether in the hands of business or government, constitute a new and sinister threat to the integrity of the individual. Novelists, therefore, have continued to be fascinated by the image of the man who lives in society but is not part of it, who while taking advantage of the social system, plays the game of life according to his own rules.

We should be quick, however, to note that the predicament of individual versus society does not necessarily equal the picaresque situation. Thomas Hardy, commenting on a critique of *Jude the Obscure*, suggests that inevitably the central conflict of a novel is generated in one of two ways, "by an opposing environment either of things inherent in the universe, or of human institutions." [3] The two kinds of conflict indicated correspond more or less to Frye's — and Hawthorne's — distinction between novel and romance. It follows, then, that almost any novel that is not a romance, any novel that gives us man in the drawing room and not man against the stormy sky, involves in some sense a conflict between the individual and his society. If this is the case, we shall have to consider what distinguishes the picaresque conflict with society. The kinds of clash between individual and collective that have been presented in the novel are numerous, and it would hardly be to the point to attempt an exhaustive survey of them here. But it may be instructive to compare briefly the picaresque situation of individual over against society with that presented in Cervantes' great archetypal novel. *Don Quixote* not only establishes the dominant pattern for the novel in general, but it is also the first great transfiguration of the picaresque novel.

The Knight of the Mournful Countenance is also a man who does not belong, a man on the move, and a man who takes things into his own hands. But there is this important difference: Don Quixote is an outsider, not because society rejects him, but because he rejects society as it is—and brings himself to see the world as it is not. And he rejects society as it is because he has culled from literature an ideal image of what society should be. At the outset of this study, we observed that one of the fundamental characteristics of the picaroon is that the scope of his imagination is limited by the boundaries of the status quo. Upon the image of the world as it presents itself to him he projects neither an image of a better society in the future nor of a better one in the past: he is neither a rebel nor a literary nostalgist. Lazarillo, like Don Quixote, is a man of imagination; but the picaro's imagination is pragmatic, the Don's idealistic. The picaresque hero observes people sharply in order to learn how to outsmart them at their own game. For his own benefit, he engages in the reprehensible practices of the world around him; he meets society on its own terms while, however, remaining apart from it and in some ways above it. The picaroon improvises his manner of acting as he goes; he preserves a strong sense of spontaneity in the way he lives. Don Quixote, on the other hand, tries to follow a pattern that he has learned from the printed page; life for him amounts to the fulfillment of a duty—both to himself and to the world. In sum, the picaroon lives by ear; Don Quixote lives by the book.

Julien Sorel, the hero of Stendhal's *Le Rouge et le Noir* (1830) and the prototype of so many figures in nineteenth-century fiction, hovers in a precarious position somewhere between Lazarillo and Don Quixote. Stendhal's favorite definition of the novel—"a novel is a mirror carried along a road" [4]—is actually a definition of the picaresque novel and of its Cervantesque transformation. Though Julien is by nature essentially—indeed, painfully— quixotic, picaresque elements play a leading part in the progress of *Le Rouge et le Noir*. Like most picaroons, Julien comes from a lower-class background but soon manages to disengage himself from class, family, and home. Stendhal, furthermore, develops rather elaborately, as he will do even more extensively with Fabrice del Dongo, the suggestion that Julien is not his father's son. The motif of illegitimate birth is one used by many picaresque novelists both to parody the mysterious birth of the traditional hero and to reinforce the impression that the protagonist is a man alone in the world, without home or progenitors, not limited in his future career by the known nature of his parents.

When Julien appears at the beginning of the novel, not yet nineteen years old, he is already a man who has made a conscious decision to act the part of a hypocrite in order to get ahead. His career consequently involves a picaresque effort of role-playing; Julien has the picaroon's mobility because he can teach himself to play the part that is called for by the situation—he can be the servant of many masters. His advance follows the picaresque path from country to city in three long, symmetrical stages: from the house of M. de Rênal to the provincial capital, Besançon, and from Besançon to the great metropolis, Paris.

In characteristic picaresque fashion, Julien is an outsider who has the knack of getting inside. But because in his thinking he remains an outsider, he maintains what we have referred to as the satiric distance of the picaroon from his world: he sees the pompousness and vulgar materialism of M. de Rênal, the hypocrisy and brute greediness of the seminarists at Besançon, the pettiness and pretentiousness of the beau monde in Paris. He has the profoundest scorn for those around him wherever he goes—his moral ideal is to be perched on an immense rock, sure of being separate from other men[5]—but he shares with his picaresque literary forebears a willingness to deal with the world on its own corrupt terms.

Julien's trouble is that his misguided quixotism prevents him from exercising the virtues or enjoying the pleasures of his picaresque calling. And Julien's tragedy is that, in contrast to Don Quixote, the literary ideal upon which he models his life is fundamentally alien to his nature. There are two books that serve Stendhal's hero as his *Amadis of Gaul:* the *Mémorial de Sainte-Hélène* and Rousseau's *Confessions.* The latter cultivates in Julien to a dangerous degree the weaknesses to which he is temperamentally inclined, while the former imposes on Julien a task which he is not really fit to undertake. From Rousseau Julien inherits an exaggerated sensibility, an "amour-propre toujours souffrant," [6] (continually afflicted self-love), a constantly smarting class consciousness. Venturing forth, picaroonlike, into the rough bump-and-bustle of the marketplace of predatory competition, he is as sensitive as a homely schoolgirl at her first prom. And in choosing Napoleon as his model, Julien sets out to become a Superior Man by following a career of ruthlessness, aggressiveness, and unprincipled scheming. In point of fact, however, he is shy, retiring, and by nature disposed to compassion for those who suffer and to gratitude toward his benefactors.

This disparity between the man and his ideal explains why Julien is always playing a role, not merely in the various attitudes of hypocrisy he assumes to deceive others, but in the whole Napoleonic stance toward the world with which he deceives himself. For Lazarillo, the career of roguery is the natural and inevitable means of getting along in the world. For Don Quixote, the pursuit of the chivalric ideal is the most congenial means of fulfillment for a need deep-seated in his nature. Julien Sorel, in contrast to both the picaro and the Don, is continually posturing; the natural features of his young face are distorted by one grimace after another. This, for example,

is the way Stendhal describes his hero at the height of
his conspiratorial extravagance, as he is about to mail off
hidden in a Bible to his friend Fouquet the love letter
he has just received from Mathilde de la Mole:

Il faut en convenir, le regard de Julien était atroce, sa
physionomie hideuse; elle respirait le crime sans alliage. C'était
l'homme malheureux en guerre avec toute la société.
Aux armes! s'écria Julien.[7]
(It must be agreed, Julien's look was atrocious, his features
were hideous; they expressed unalloyed crime. He was the
unfortunate individual at war with all of society.
"To arms!" Julien cried out.)

There are rare moments when Julien manages to forget
"son triste rôle de plébeien révolté"[8] (his unhappy role
of plebeian in revolt) and enjoys the success he has won.
But, for the most part, life remains for him a duty, the
performance of which forces him repeatedly to summon
up all his will power. Consequently, despite the crucial
importance of the detailed social background in *Le Rouge
et le Noir,* the most central dramatic conflict takes place
within Julien Sorel; in the last analysis, Stendhal has substituted a fluoroscope for the picaresque mirror-on-the-
road. Julien is an unhappier creature by far than either
of his ancestors from Spanish fiction; but, for precisely
this reason, his story has a psychological fascination that
theirs could not have.

The picaresque ritual of learning the ways of the
world is present in *Le Rouge et le Noir:* there are even
a few completely traditional instances of it, as when the
young Julien has his pocket picked by a friendly stranger
as soon as he arrives in Paris for the first time. But picaresque loss of innocence has been transformed in this
novel, as in the latter part of *Gil Blas,* into a process of
growing moral awareness. Julien comes to see more clearly
not only the world around him but himself as well. In

prison, after the shattering of the final, momentary illusion that he has succeeded in making himself M. le chevalier Julien Sorel de la Vernaye, he finally discovers the disastrous incompatibility of his ideal both with the world as it is and with his own nature. *Le Rouge et le Noir* has taken a picaresque situation as the background for a drama of inner experience: the literary prospect visible from Julien's cell window is not new roads unfurling but the cloistered agony of consciousness of an Emma Bovary or a Raskolnikov.

In Thackeray's *Barry Lyndon* (1844), on the other hand, we find a writer looking back with nostalgia, despite his Victorian better judgment, on the departed Age of the Picaresque, and attempting to re-create that age. *The Memoirs of Barry Lyndon, Esq.* offers an interesting example of a novel that succeeds brilliantly where its author may not have meant it to succeed, and falters only when the writer is actually carrying out his intended purpose. In the battle waged by *Fraser's Magazine* in the early 1840's against the then popular Newgate School of English fiction, Thackeray's stand was unequivocal: a rogue was a rogue, and any writer who glorified criminality was himself worthy of censure. What would appear to be the original conception behind *Barry Lyndon* is founded upon a black-and-white morality alien both to the eighteenth century and to the picaresque novel: a scoundrel, relating his exploits in a tone of overbearing conceit, would gradually show himself to be a dastardly scoundrel. In general strategy, Thackeray seems to follow Fielding's *Jonathan Wild*. His moral scheme, however, is simpler than that of *Jonathan Wild;* for Fielding does not merely set up a scoundrel to knock down, but uses his scoundrel to focus a satirical attack on predatory "greatness" wherever it appears in society.

Fortunately for Thackeray's novel, his moralistic aim

is not fully realized until the last hundred pages of the book. Before that point, what makes *Barry Lyndon* such a remarkable re-creation of the picaresque novel is its author's ability to identify imaginatively with his protagonist and even to evoke sympathy for him. Thackeray —because he was a man of curiously divided allegiances which he himself scarcely recognized—presents an instructive object lesson in what can happen to the picaresque novel when it encounters the alien spirit of a later period. Were Thackeray more typical of his age, he would have seen the opportunistic outsider merely as a cad, as in fact he intended to see him, and his novel would not have been a picaresque novel at all. For a writer and a reading public that hold sacred some strict ideal of social conformity and propriety, the picaresque novel is no longer a real possibility. But *Barry Lyndon* is such a revealing document precisely because there existed in the Victorian Thackeray certain underground connections with an older, picaresque ethic; consequently, this novel of his—like much of *Vanity Fair* itself—gives us a vigorously imagined picaresque world which is however impinged upon by a more orthodox and socially dutiful vision.

There are some interesting affinities between Thackeray, the would-be moralist, and this archrogue that he has created. The journalist-novelist who always insisted on his status as a gentleman and was nearly always insecure about it,[9] could well understand Barry's megalomaniac desire constantly to affirm his dubious nobility. Thackeray was just as familiar with the addiction to the gaming table which is the livelihood and ruin of his hero; he himself had gambled away more than half his patrimony. And it is hardly a coincidence that Thackeray, who remained a faithfully Oedipal son to his mother till his dying day, gives us a rogue who is the object of the slavish devotions of a mother all his life, and who is made to conclude that "these [mothers] are the only women who never deceive a man, and whose affection remains constant through all trials." [10]

The adventurous eighteenth-century world, moreover, in which Barry Lyndon lives, is one that appeals immensely to Thackeray. Looking back from a mid-nineteenth-century viewpoint, Thackeray sees in the earlier period an age when life was dangerous and challenging, not humdrum, when daring skill, not base mercantile virtues, enabled a man to excel. "None but men of courage and genius could live and prosper in a society where every one was bold and clever." The illustrious Mr. Lyndon, supposedly writing in 1814, repeatedly laments the passing of the brave world he knew in his youth; the Irish rogue's eulogies of the departed picaresque age are among the finest passages in the book, and Thackeray must have held them very close to heart. In the earlier age, there were significant distinctions between classes; aristocracy lived as became it in brilliant dress and grand gesture. In the grey present age, social distinctions had been leveled into flat and universal mediocrity by the stolid bourgeoisie. "It is a conspiracy of the middle classes against gentlemen: it is only the shopkeeper cant which is to go down nowadays." In the century past, life was leisurely yet varied; there was always time for a new companion, a new tale, a new experience. In this latter day, everyone is swept along in a single-minded business-like rush.

> There was much more liveliness and bustle on the king's highroad in those times, than in these days of stagecoaches, which carry you from one end of the kingdom to another in a few score hours. The gentry rode their own horses or drove in their own coaches, and spent three days on a journey which now occupies ten hours; so that there was no lack of company for a person travelling towards Dublin.[11]

Had Barry Lyndon lived a generation later, he undoubtedly would have substituted "railway" for "stage coach." But his comment is in any case just one step away from the explanation for the decline of the picaresque novel offered by Walter Allen. "The railways killed the picaresque novel. It had been an admirably flexible form for the portrayal of contrasting social classes: the road cut a cross section through national life. But the coach, and pedestrianism for those who could not afford the coach, gave way before the train with its first-, second-, and third-class compartments, its much greater speed and its much greater cheapness." [12]

Now young Barry Lyndon (or Redmond Barry, as he is first called) is, to begin with, really no worse than the world to which he belongs, despite Thackeray's intention to set him up as a model of infamy. The one flagrant sin of which he is guilty at the outset of his career is his immense egotism; this fault renders him bizarre but hardly detestable. Barry is a literary hybrid, a cross between the picaroon and the *miles gloriosus,* and the extravagances of his conceit are not without a certain charm. We smile indulgently at the lovesick adolescent Barry with his fantastical notions of romance or at the kidnapped recruit Barry stoutly affirming to his captors his descent from the noble kings of Ireland. The fact is that as long as Barry remains the underdog, his fierce snap and his loud bark are likely to inspire only sympathy. Like any good picaroon, Thackeray's hero is victimized in a variety of ways when he sets out into the world: by Capt. and Mrs. Fitzsimons, the couple that takes him in at Dublin in more than one sense; by Fakenham, the surly, callow army lieutenant; by the crimp who shanghais him into Frederick's army; by Potzdorff, the scheming Prussian officer whom he serves in Berlin. Young Barry must learn some hard lessons from a hard world. If he enunciates his ethic as "*à la guerre c'est à la guerre*, and I am none of your milksops," [18] it is quite true that he finds himself *à la guerre*, at war, both literally and figuratively.

In the first three quarters of *Barry Lyndon*, while the protagonist is still leading the life of a picaroon, the narrative is colorfully episodic in true picaresque fashion: we feel a continuing interest not only in Barry's exploits but in the large and varied panorama of men, manners, and morals that serves as a background for the hero's adventures. But once Barry has succeeded in his "courtship" and has obtained the hand and land of Lady Lyndon, the tenor of the novel changes completely. For nearly a hundred pages we are made to witness the same oppressive scene: a brutal and selfish man tyrannizing over a silly but nevertheless helpless and innocent woman. Barry Lyndon has exchanged the costume of the vagabond rogue for that of the villain of nineteenth-century melodrama, stalking around his ill-gotten estate, his fierce mustaches bristling, a whiskey bottle in each pocket and a horsewhip in his hand.

This peculiar failure of imagination in the last section of *Barry Lyndon* is symptomatic of the general ambivalence or uncertainty of attitude that mars Thackeray's work. Thackeray was in many ways more at home in the eighteenth century than in his own age, but he lacked the firmness of moral purpose to be a really dissident spirit. Part of his mind remained enslaved to a century that was profoundly uncongenial to it. A talent like Thackeray's might have produced a great picaresque novel; as it is, he managed to sail through fifteen chapters of sparkling picaresque narrative before he foundered on the rock of his Victorian solid moral purpose.

But forty years later, and some four thousand miles further to the west, the picaresque tradition was to realize a kind of apotheosis in Mark Twain's *Huckleberry Finn*.

It has recently been argued that Huck should not be considered a picaroon at all. As Wallace Stegner states the position, Huck cannot be called a picaro because "he is neither callous nor uncommitted; he does not glance off experience, or prey on it, but is absorbed by it, wrung by it, enlarged by it . . . He has no virtues except the essential ones, and most of the vices except the unforgivable ones." [14] Mr. Stegner's words reflect an admirable understanding of Huck Finn at the same time that they slight the picaresque novel and the range of moral possibilities offered by it. For, as we have seen through a number of different examples, the picaresque novel as a rule attempts to unsettle preconceived notions of what a rogue is and seeks to force its readers to make the critical distinction between rogue and scoundrel. The picaroon—at his best—is precisely the man who, in Mr. Stegner's happy formulation, "has no virtues except the essential ones and most of the vices except the unforgivable ones." Viewed against the background of the picaresque tradition, Huckleberry Finn is an embodiment of all the virtues potential in the distinctively picaresque situation.

Huck is admittedly not callous, but he has enough of the picaroon's thick skin to prevent experience from paralyzing him or torturing him excessively. The same Huck who can fear for a murderer's life or quake for his own safety is able to administer to himself the bracing warning that "it warn't no time to be sentimentering." He does not prey on experience or glance off it, but he does enjoy it immensely whenever he can, which is very much what the picaroon tries to do in life. If Huck is committed, it is only to be faithful to the impulses of his own heart; and this is a kind of commitment that' would not be alien to Lazarillo de Tormes or to Gil Blas or to almost any member of the picaresque clan. If Huck's moral awareness is unusually alive and unusually sensitive, it is due in large part to the peculiar picaresque position of outsider-on-the-inside to which he has been born. Companionship and affection play a very important part in Huck's life, and consequently human beings are valuable creatures in his eyes. And, as an orphaned, half-outcast "loner," he understands the pain of being alone, the terror of being unprotected, the distress of being victimized. The lowest of the low on the white's social scale, "brung up to wickedness," Huck can feel empathy even for those whom society would condemn out of hand. "I begun to think how dreadful it was, even for murderers, to be in such a fix. I says to myself, there ain't no telling but I might come to be a murderer myself yet, and then how would I like it?" [15] Huck Finn, in short, is a paragon of the picaresque virtue of compassion that begins with Lazarillo himself.

In characteristic picaresque fashion, Huck would not dream of rebelling against the society to which he cannot fully belong; his keen boy's eyes are never clouded by the venom of hatred or embitterment. Like little Lazaro, he accepts without question what tradition has taught him is right; the contrast between the pedestrianism of his "conscience" and the acuteness of his moral instinct gives his story one of its important satiric perspectives. And though Huck is sometimes a fool, he can also be very shrewd, so that he is capable of sharp satiric observation from his vantage point in-and-out of society. "There warn't anybody at the church, except mabe a hog or two, for there warn't any lock on the door, and hogs like a puncheon floor in summertime because it's cool. If you notice, most folks don't go to church only when they've got to; but a hog is different." [16]

Perhaps you might not notice, but you can depend upon it that Huck would. He has not been "brung up" to church-going, but he also has had to sweat out many a tedious Sunday morning in a hard pew; he knows what it's all about, and at the same time he can look at it with a healthy detachment.

Huck stands in the picaroon's median position between the respectable world and the criminal world; he is himself sounder than either, and he can observe the vices of each and the falseness and pretensions shared by both. Under the greasy thumb of the Duke and King, Huck is precisely in the predicament of Gil Blas in the robbers' cave. Huck perched in the tree watching the spectacle of mutual slaughter of the Grangerford-Shepherdson feud plays the same role of observer as Gil Blas at the Spanish court viewing another kind of mad dog fight, though, in contrast to Huck, the Hispano-French picaroon is himself temporarily drawn into the madness.

Huck does not trouble himself much about purely formal definitions of truth or honesty: he is not averse to "borrowing" a watermelon, and he will spin a dozen fantastic yarns about himself for the sheer fun of it, if he has no better reason. Like his picaresque forebears, he has recognized that the respectable world pays only lip service to the ideal of strict veracity which it neglects at least as much as he does. "I never seen anybody but lied one time or another." [17] But Huck remains loyal to the truth of his own humane instincts; the moral stance he takes is a realization of the possibility of absolute integrity implicit in the picaresque rejection of society's hypocrisies.

And *Huckleberry Finn* is a more perfect work of art than any of the traditional picaresque novels because in it Mark Twain has fashioned a language completely appropriate to the ideal of individual integrity embodied by his hero. In terms of literary tradition, the language of *Huckleberry Finn* substituted living speech for the tired, bookish diction prevalent in American literature a century ago. But more to the point, in terms of the novel itself as an organic structure, *Huckleberry Finn's* language mirrors with perfect fidelity the moral condition of its picaresque protagonist: it is the language people really speak, not the one books pretend they speak; it is, in its very freedom from school rules and formalism, a language that reports experience more precisely and reproduces it more honestly. As a faithful linguistic expression of all that is morally sound in the picaresque code, one could hardly have asked for more.

We have already observed that as the art of fiction became more complex and more sophisticated, it grew increasingly unlikely that anyone would be able to write a "pure" picaresque novel. One of the reasons that *Huckleberry Finn* is a closer approach to the picaresque than most novels of its time or ours is that it deals with boyhood. A boy's life, of course, is not necessarily simple: the moral seriousness and complexity of Mark Twain's novel should easily convince us of that. But because Huck is a boy—and we cannot imagine him as ever being anything but a boy—there are distinct limits to the kind of transformation he can undergo and to the order of problematic reality he can sense. When, on the other hand, a modern writer undertakes to relate the picaresque career of a grown man, his task is more likely to be complicated by the fact that he has the awareness of a modern writer. A case in point is Saul Bellow's attempt to adopt the picaresque form to the novelistic idiom of mid-twentieth century in *The Adventures of Augie March* (1953).

Chicago-bred Augie is a servant of so many masters that, by comparison, Lazarillo and Guzman are mere Iberian stick-in-the-muds. From the end of the Roaring Twenties in Chicago to the years following World War II in Europe, Augie gets himself involved in every occupation—legiti-

mate, semilegitimate, and illegitimate—from dog-training
and shoplifting to lizard-hunting and the merchant marine.
For the central theme that Bellow has drawn from the
picaresque tradition is the picaroon's unquenchable thirst
for experience, for a continual variety and multiplicity of
experience. Augie tries everywhere to be "first to knock,
first admitted," [18] as he tells us at the very outset of his
story.

This limitless curiosity about a very large and complex
world is both a major strength and a weakness in *Augie
March.* The picaresque panorama of this novel is as rich
and varied as we could hope to find, but like one of those
encyclopedic canvasses by Brueghel or Bosch, it is also
somewhat bewildering in its richness. The kind of sentence
Augie characteristically uses in his narrative reflects the
structural problem of the novel as a whole. Augie is constantly reaching out in his language for more details, more
descriptive adjectives, more particulars of experience. His
sentences typically are Whitmanesque catalogues, crammed
full and overflowing with vitality, but also tending to be
top-heavy and to sprawl, leading us to forget where we
started or where we are headed. This, for example, is how
he describes one of his early jobs:

> But it was the figure you cut as an employee, on an em-
> ployee's footing with the girls, in work clothes, and being of
> that tin-tough, creaking, jazzy bazaar of hardware, glassware,
> chocolate, chickenfeed, jewelry, drygoods, oilcloth, and song
> hits—that was the big thing; and even being the Atlases of it,
> under the floor, hearing how the floor bore up under the ambling
> weight of hundreds, with the fanning, breathing movie organ
> next door and the rumble descending from the trolleys on
> Chicago Avenue . . .[19]

And on the sentence goes.

The key to Augie's approach to life is the fact that he
refers to the world he lives in as "the multiverse." [20] He

wants no part of systems and systematizers that seek to unify experience under a single embracing pattern. In an age of specialization and compartmentalization, he refuses to be thrust into any one pigeonhole. His story illustrates an aspect of the literary myth of the picaroon which is particularly appealing for the modern world. In a society where most people spend their productive hours repeating the same limited acts, forever incomplete in themselves, the picaroon is an individual who can do and be whatever he wants. In this respect, the picaroon is a parallel, within society, to Robinson Crusoe, outside of it. Crusoe offers an imaginative escape from the specialization of an industrialized world by recapitulating the basic activities of civilization, by being all things to himself. The picaroon represents another possibility of escape in his ability to be anything while refusing to be one thing in particular. Augie himself points out the analogy and contrast between him and Crusoe. "Crusoe, alone and with nature, under heaven, had a busy, complicated time of it with the unhuman itself, and I am in a crowd that yields results with much more difficulty and reluctance and am part of it myself." [21]

Like the traditional picaroon, Augie is an inveterate displaced person. He has no home, no calling, no sure set of values. He is moved by the picaresque impulse to assume responsibility for his own life, to make himself master of his own fate. And so he stubbornly refuses to let other people determine the course of his existence. "Why should I turn into one of those people who didn't know who they themselves were?" [22] While the traditional picaroon is often an appealing fellow, particularly for women, one of Augie's distinctive characteristics is his curious attractiveness both for men and for women. Because of it, he is far more often befriended than victimized. Augie is constantly falling into the company of self-appointed teachers, theoreticians, people who want to make experience conform to some ideal. But his own attitude toward the world is the picaresque attitude—empirical and pragmatic, attempting to deal directly with the facts of experience without any intervening preinterpretation.

And yet Augie March is not altogether a picaresque hero. What has happened in Saul Bellow's novel is that the picaresque rootlessness, wandering, desire for multiplicity and diversity of experience, have been used as the vehicle for a *Bildungsroman,* a novelistic search for the true self. "I have always tried to become what I am," [23] Augie tells us. Bellow's protagonist generally deceives himself more than he is deceived by others precisely because of this groping for identity which is the core of his story. In the traditional picaresque novel, on the other hand, the hero already is what he is; sometimes splendidly, sometimes ignominiously, but always confidently, he is himself.

Unlike the genuine picaroon, Augie does not seek experience for its own sake but rather as a means for finding himself. Consequently his journey, particularly in the later chapters of the book, is arduous and painful with few of the picaresque roadside pleasures and not much of the picaresque sense of delight. As Augie grows older, his feeling of unrest and dissatisfaction grows as well, for he wants very much to be straight on "the axial lines of life" and he never seems to manage it. The real picaroon, on the other hand, has a kind of gyroscope built into him; it is one of his most distinctive characteristics that he remains on the axial lines of life, however rough the tempest-tossing to which life subjects him. Huck Finn is an impressive example of this particular faculty. But in Augie's case, "hard, hard work" [24] is always going on inside, work that is sometimes harrowing and never completed.

One of the problematic aspects of Bellow's book is the conflict between Augie's deadly serious struggle to be himself and the general picaresque conception of this novel.

Augie ends his story with a fine picaresque flourish: in response to what could be painful or pitiful, Augie breaks into a grin.

That's the *animal ridens* in me, the laughing creature, forever rising up. What's so laughable, that a Jacqueline, for instance, as hard used as that by rough forces, will still refuse to lead a disappointed life? Or is the laugh at nature—including eternity— that it thinks it can win over us and the power of hope? Nah, nah! I think. It never well. But that is the joke, on one or the other, and laughing is an enigma that includes both.[25]

The passage in itself is an admirable statement of the heroism of the picaresque stance toward a hard and unsympathetic world. But for a large part of the narrative that precedes, Augie March has been far from the laughing and laughable creature that the picaroon should see in himself, and this final statement is therefore not quite so convincing as it ought to be.

And yet the magic of the picaroon's unalloyed delight in living is not entirely beyond the imaginative grasp of the modern novelist: within a year after the publication of *Augie March,* Thomas Mann was to offer to the reading public his brilliant venture into the picaresque, *Bekenntnisse des Hochstaplers Felix Krull.* Mann had begun the story of his archimposter in 1911, and if it took him more than forty years to finish the first part of this still incomplete novel, it is perhaps because such a book could only be written in a holiday mood, and for a writer like Mann, of whom life seemed to demand such hard soul work, the imagination could be spared little time off for holidays. But throughout his career, Mann was fascinated by the archetype of the trickster; there is more than a touch of the picaroon in his Joseph. It is therefore not surprising that this one expressly picaresque effort of his—suggested by the real-life confessions of the Roumanian swindler Manolescue —proved to be extraordinarily fruitful: the picaresque novel opened to Mann possibilities of expression which were ordinarily closed to him, and, on the other hand, Mann's treatment of the genre made vividly clear an important aspect of the picaresque nature generally more latent than apparent.

It hardly needs to be said that what Mann does in *Felix Krull* is to play in a picaresque key the dominant theme of his career as a novelist—the distinctiveness of the artist, the ineradicable difference between him and other men. In most of Mann's work, of course, this difference makes itself felt in a painful isolation of the creative individual, in a profound antagonism between the artist and the society in which he lives. The picaresque novel, on the other hand, presents the possibility of an individual who, though never really part of society, is not at odds with it. If the author of *Tonio Kröger* generally saw the artist as Yeats imagined Keats—standing on the outside, with his nose pressed against the sweetshop window—the picaresque novel could teach Mann how to create a Felix Krull who early masters the art of letting himself inside the store to fill his pockets with sweets.

Felix, as a good picaroon, has an immense love of life and a gift of perpetual responsiveness to the pleasures life offers. The world in general, and society in particular, are accomplished facts of existence which he does not question—in picaresque fashion, he merely tries to make the most of them. When his first employer asks him if he is a socialist, Felix can answer with honest enthusiasm, "Nicht doch, Herr Generaldirektor! Ich finde die Gesellschaft reizend, so wie sie ist, und brenne darauf, ihre Gunst zu gewinnen." (Certainly not, Herr Generaldirektor! I find society charming just the way it is, and I am burning to win its favor.") In the career of this charming confidence man, the problematic tension between life and art has disappeared because life itself has become the arena of artistic endeavor. All the daily activities most people perform in shambling, slipshod ways are artistic challenges for Felix: it is an art to serve a cup of tea correctly, or to wear proper evening dress, or to make love. But Krull is even more an artist in his constant role as illusionist. He himself is the raw material of this art, or rather, since his is a performing art, he himself together with his audience. "Wer die Welt recht liebt, der bildet sich ihr gefällig." [26] ("He who truly loves the world shapes himself to be pleasing to it.")

Krull makes it clear, moreover, that though he regards himself as an infinitely plastic creature, he molds himself to use the world and does not let the world mold him for its own use. Mann's hero preserves the advantageous duality of the picaresque relationship toward society—he is in it, enjoying it, and outside it, observing it with critical (and satirical) detachment.

Ich kann mein inneres Verhalten zur Welt, oder zur Gesellschaft, nicht anders als widerspruchvoll bezeichnen. Bei allen Verlangen nach Liebesaustausch mit ihr eignete ihm nicht selten eine sinnende Kühle, eine Neigung zu abschätzender Betrachtung, die mich selbst in Erstaunen setzte.[27]

(I can only describe my essential attitude to the world, or to society, as contradictory. With all my desire to be on affectionate terms with the world, I was often aware of a deliberate coolness, a tendency in me to critical observation, which astonished me.)

It should be evident enough how this novel of Mann's, by casting a picaroon as the artist, is able to escape the magic circle of tormented introspection that usually imprisons Mann's artists. But *Felix Krull* would not have been the successful novel it is if the idea of the hero as artist were merely a preoccupation of the author pasted onto the picaresque conventions. In point of fact, Mann has exploited in his characterization of a rogue an element essential to the picaresque nature. The picaroon, as we have observed in a wide variety of instances, is a man of imagination. It is only because of his imagination that he can get along so well in what is, after all, a precariously marginal existence. It is his imagination that enables him to be a nimble deceiver, a protean role-player and master of disguise, a man infinitely adaptable to swiftly changing circumstances. As Felix reminds the Marquis Venosta when they decide to exchange roles, "Kleider machen Leute, Marquis,—oder besser umgekehrt: Der Mann macht das Kleid." [28] ("Clothes make the man, Marquis—or rather, the other way around: the man makes the clothes.") Disguise is not simply a matter of costume; it takes a man with imagination to wear the costume well and to make it believable.

The picaroon, in his aspect of master-of-his-fate, actually handles experience much the way an artist handles the materials of his art. To the ordinary man things happen; for him most of the components of experience are, to use the Aristotelian distinction, already actual, just as lines, shapes, textures, and colors are simply actual to someone who will never be a painter. But experience for the opportunist picaroon—like the elements of the visual world for the painter—is always predominantly potential (which is another reason why picaresque novels have no endings). The ingenious rogue, like the artist, selects elements from experience as it presents itself to him and reconstitutes them in a new order that suits his own purposes. Felix Krull, as the product of a sophisticated and self-conscious age, is more aware of the artistic side of his calling than any of his picaresque predecessors. But Lazarillo, for all his relative crudeness and simplicity, exercised the same profession: illusionism and manipulation as a kind of art are vitally present in the picaresque tradition from its very beginnings.

In *Felix Krull* Mann has utilized the artistic aspect of the rogue with great conscious care. Indeed, there are points in the novel when one feels that the rogue is employed almost symbolically to stand for the artist: in this quasi-symbolic use of the hero, Mann's treatment of the picaresque material is perhaps most distinctively modern. On the other hand, there is a long-standing tradition in Western literature which inverts the terms of the equation suggested by *Felix Krull:* at least as far back as Boccaccio's Bruno and Buffalmacco, writers on occasion have chosen to present the artist as a rogue or trickster. In the literature of our own age, then, concerned as it has been with the tension between the artist and society, it is hardly surprising that a novelist should be attracted to elaborate upon this traditional conception of the artist as picaroon. This is precisely what Joyce Cary has done in *The Horse's Mouth* (1944), his lively account of the ups and jolting downs of the painter Gulley Jimson.

Having already considered what the picaresque hero has in common with the artist, we might for a moment note what the artist has in common with the picaroon. If the rogue borrows from the artist something of his profes-sional method, the artist assumes much the same peculiar social standing as the rogue. The artist—ideally, at any rate—is, like the picaresque hero, an individual of unusual worth who can never seriously hope to be properly acknowledged by society. Like the picaroon, the artist cannot be set down as an out-and-out criminal, yet the activity in which he engages remains profoundly suspect in the eyes of the respectable world. And rightly so, as Gulley Jimson reminds us several times: for nothing could undermine comfortable habit, convention, propriety, tradition, more than an honest modern art. As a man dedicated to working on his own version of the truth, the artist is not likely to be awed by the kind of "truth" embodied in law or custom. But however great a heretic he may be, if the artist wants paint on his palette and bread in his belly, he cannot easily afford either to wage open war on society or to turn his back on it. One path

open to him is that which is trod upon by the picaresque
hero: to live the best he can off a society to which he
does not belong while still preserving his integrity as an
individual.

For most artists, however, this is a piece of tightrope
walking which it is not so easy to execute. The sensitivity
that generally accompanies the artistic temperament
makes it painful or maddening for the typical artist to
live in a world that abuses him and that is blind to the
values so important to him. But it is in the face of just
this difficulty that Gulley Jimson can call on a picaresque
resource which not only prevents life from defeating him
but which enables him to become a great comic figure—
that is, a character who is not merely funny but who,
like Falstaff or Sam Weller, makes us feel that there is
no room for tragedy in life. Gulley's great picaresque
resource is toughness, or, to be more precise, toughness
and resilience. "We all know what the world is," says
Gulley, and every picaroon from the Spanish Renaissance
on would heartily second him. "Free for all. And the
winner is the chap who gets knocked out first and comes
to while the others are still asleep." [29]

Gulley Jimson's toughness is not simply the result of
naturally sinewy moral fiber; it derives from a conscious
resolution on his part not to let life break him, not to
take life too seriously. Gulley differs from the traditional
picaroon chiefly in the consciousness with which he takes
this stand. But in any case, he has the remarkable picaresque faculty of regarding life as a game. To be sure,
it is a rough, serious game for Gulley: one might say, a
body-contact game that leaves bruises with a real ache.
But because he has this sense of the game, Gulley can
manage to substitute mere opponents for what could be
enemies; an opponent can break your skin, but he can't
get under it, the way an enemy might. One of the distinctive features of the picaresque hero is his attitude as

a sturdy, competitive fighter without rancor, an outcast who does not imagine society as his enemy. He can be abused without feeling persecuted, unfortunate without feeling sorry for himself. Like any intelligent player in a tough game, his face is always set toward the possibilities of the future and not toward the disappointments of the past.

It is this picaresque stance of gamesmanship that makes it possible for Gulley Jimson to persist in his art and in his enjoyment of life no matter how drastic the setbacks he suffers. He does not permit himself the luxury of hating the "Boorjoys" whose world has thwarted him— that would be bad for the digestion. So he can have the pleasure of regarding them with healthy scorn, or even with amused tolerance. Because Gulley preserves the picaroon's equanimity in accepting people for what they are—whether tight-laced burghers or indulgent millionaires—he can remain an entertained observer at the spectacle of life. And what is more important, it leaves his mind free to concentrate on art. For Gulley's relationship to art is in several ways analogous to the relationship of the picaroon to experience in general. His art tries him sorely, sometimes threatens to confound him, but it is his great source of joy, and he can never be done with it. To Gulley in his art as to the picaroon in his adventures, past achievement is of no interest—it is the present challenge that attracts him. The world is good because there are always new paintings to undertake, just as for the picaroon there are always new experiences to be lived. "Certainly an artist has no right to complain of his fate. For he has great pleasures. To start new pictures." [30]

Gulley, like the traditional picaroon and like the poet, as many view him, is an eternal adolescent. In fact, the optimism of his adolescent eagerness is sometimes detrimental to him, for he learns less about the wily ways of the world than most picaresque heroes, and his ingenious confidence games or his ventures into pilfering most often end him up in a prison cell or a hospital bed. But perhaps this lack of deftness is simply due to the fact that Gulley's imaginative powers are focused primarily on his painting and not on his rogueries. In any case, Joyce Cary's artist is the memorable comic character he is because in both the naïveté of his scheming and the boldness of his painting, he has the unique ability of the gamesman-picaroon to wake every day as though it were the first day of his life. When Coker, catching Gulley overusing an old dodge for free drinks, asks him whether he has a birthday every day, the painter can answer honestly, "Yes, every day's my birthday. Often twice a day. Due to art." [31]

Gulley Jimson, in sum, is a worthy successor to the great picaroons because he embodies the distinctive heroism and hedonism of the picaresque anti-heroic attitude. He is an *animal ridens,* as Augie March would have liked to be, and at the same time he can see in himself an *animal risible* ("grinning like a gargoyle" [32]), in the most admirable manner of Gil Blas. Laughter for Gulley—and for the picaresque hero in general—amounts to a courageous affirmation, almost a form of devotion. It is his refusal to take himself or life too seriously, his refusal to be choked by rancor, his refusal to become anything less than the observer, the appreciator, the enjoyer, anything less than the man who is capable of the miracle of daily rebirth. No picaroon could want a finer last hour than Gulley achieves as he is rushed to the hospital in an ambulance under the solicitous care of a nun. Gulley, as usual, has been talking, and the nun tries to quiet him. " 'It's dangerous for you to talk, you're seriously ill.' 'Not so seriously as you're well. How don't you enjoy life, mother. I should laugh all round my neck at this minute if my shirt wasn't a bit on the tight side.' 'It would be better for you to pray.' 'Same thing, mother.' " [33]

WORKS CITED
NOTES · INDEX

WORKS CITED

Allen, Walter. *The English Novel.* New York: E. P. Dutton and
  Co., 1954.
Auerbach, Erich. *Mimesis: The Representation of Reality in
  Western Literature.* Translated by Willard Trask. Prince-
  ton, N.J.: Princeton University Press, 1953.
Baker, E. A. *The History of the English Novel.* 9 vols. London:
  H. F. and G. Witherly, 1929.
Bellow, Saul. *The Adventures of Augie March.* New York: The
  Viking Press, 1953.
Cary, Joyce. *The Horse's Mouth.* New York: Harper and
  Brothers, 1944.
Castro, Americo. *The Structure of Spanish History.* Princeton:
  Princeton University Press, 1954.
Cervantes, Miguel de. *Don Quixote de la Mancha.* Translated
  by Thomas Shelton. 3 vols. London: Macmillan and Co.,
  1908.
Chandler, F. W. *The Literature of Roguery.* 2 vols. Boston
  and New York: Houghton, Mifflin and Co., 1907.
Defoe, Daniel. *The Fortunes and Misfortunes of the Famous
  Moll Flanders.* Introduction by G. H. Maynadier. 2 vols.
  Boston: The University Press, 1903.
Fielding, Henry. *The History of the Adventures of Joseph
  Andrews and of His Friend Mr. Abraham Adams.* Intro-
  duction and notes by Maynard Mack. (Rinehart Editions,
  No. 15.) New York: Rinehart and Co., 1948.
——— *The History of Tom Jones. A Foundling.* Introduction
  by George Sherburn. (Modern Library, No. 185.) New
  York: Random House, 1950.
Forster, E. M. *Aspects of the Novel.* New York: Harcourt,
  Brace, and Co., 1927.
Frye, Northrop. *Anatomy of Criticism.* Princeton: Princeton
  University Press, 1957.
George, Charles H. and Katherine. *The Protestant Mind of the
  English Reformation: 1570–1640.* Princeton: Princeton
  University Press, 1961.

Gide, André. *Interviews Imaginaires.* New York: Pantheon Press, 1943.

Grieg, J. Y. T. *Thackeray, A Reconsideration.* London: Oxford University Press, 1950.

Guillén, Claudio. "The Anatomies of Roguery." Unpublished dissertation, Harvard University, 1953.

Hardy, Florence Emily. *The Later Years of Thomas Hardy.* New York: The Macmillan Company, 1930.

Humphreys, A. R. "Fielding's Irony: Its Methods and Effects," *Review of English Studies,* 18 (1942): 183–197.

Hutchens, Eleanor N. "The Identification of Irony," *ELH,* 27 (1960): 352–363.

Knights, L. C. *Drama and Society in the Age of Jonson.* London: Chatto and Windus, 1936.

Lanson, Gustave. *Histoire Illustrée de la Littérature Française.* Vol. II. Paris: Hachette et Compagnie, 1926.

Lazarillo de Tormes. Introduction by Americo Castro. Madison, Wis.: University of Wisconsin Press, 1948.

Lazarillo de Tormes, The Pleasaunte Historie of. Translated by David Rowland, London, 1586. Edited with notes by J. E. V. Crofts. Reprinted, Oxford: B. Blackwell, 1924.

Lesage, Alain-René. *Histoire de Gil Blas de Santillane.* Introduction and notes by Maurice Bardon. 2 vols. Paris: Editions Garnier Frères, 1955.

Lewis, R. W. B. *The Picaresque Saint.* Philadelphia: Lippincott, 1959.

Lintilhac, Eugène. *Lesage.* Paris: Hachette et Compagnie, 1893.

Mann, Thomas. *Gesammelte Werke.* Vol. VII: *Bekenntnisse des Hochstaplers Felix Krull.* Oldenburg, Germany: S. Fischer Verlag, 1960.

Ortega y Gassett, José. "Notes on the Novel," *The Dehumanization of Art and Other Writngs on Art and Culture.* (Anchor Books, No. A72.) Garden City, N.Y.: Doubleday and Co., 1956.

Paulson, Ronald. "Satire in the Early Novels of Smollett," *Journal of English and Germanic Philology,* 59 (1960): 381–402.

Peacham, Henry. *The Worth of a Peny or a Caution to Keep Money.* London: privately printed, 1647.

Plumb, J. H. *England in the Eighteenth Century.* (Penguin Books, No. A231.) London: Penguin Books, 1950.

Reynolds, Joshua. *Discourses on Art.* San Marino, Calif.: Huntington Library, 1959.

Smollett, Tobias. *The Adventures of Peregrine Pickle.* 3 vols. Introduction by G. H. Maynadier. Cambridge, Mass.: The University Press, 1903.

——— *The Adventures of Roderick Random.* 3 vols. Introduction by G. H. Maynadier. Cambridge, Mass.: The University Press, 1902.

——— *Letters.* Edited by E. S. Noyes. Cambridge, Mass.: Harvard University Press, 1926.

Stendhal (Henri Beyle). *Le Rouge et le Noir, Chronique du XIXe Siècle.* Edited with introduction and notes by Henri Martineau. Bourges, France: Editions Garnier Frères, 1960.

Strauss, Albrecht. "On Smollett's Language," *Style in Prose Fiction.* Edited by Harold C. Martin. New York: Columbia University Press, 1959. Pages 25–54.

Thackeray, William Makepeace. *The Memoirs of Barry Lyndon, Esq.* New York: Charles Scribner's Sons, 1904.

Twain, Mark (Samuel Clemens). *The Adventures of Huckleberry Finn.* Introduction by Wallace Stegner. (Laurel Editions.) New York: Dell Publishing Co., 1960.

Watt, Ian. *The Rise of the Novel.* Berkeley and Los Angeles: University of California Press, 1957.

Weber, Max. *The Protestant Ethic and the Spirit of Capitalism.* Translated by Talcott Parsons. New York: Charles Scribner's Sons, 1958.

Woolf, Virginia. *The Common Reader.* London: Hogarth Press, 1929.

NOTES

I. LAZARILLO AND THE PICARESQUE CODE

1. *The Pleasaunte Historie of Lazarillo de Tormes,* trans. David Rowland (London, 1586); edited with notes by J. E. V. Crofts (reprinted ed.; Oxford: B. Blackwell, 1924), p. 28. All textual references are to this edition. In every case, the passage cited has been compared with the original Spanish text.

2. Claudio Guillén, "The Anatomies of Roguery" (unpub. diss., Harvard University, 1953), p. 383.

3. *Lazarillo,* p. 11.

4. *Ibid.,* p. 12.

5. *Lazarillo* in fact bristles with stylistic aggression toward the accepted order, but it is all on the part of a knowing author working through the medium of a much more simple-minded protagonist. Lazaro himself is an instrument for irony, not an ironist.

6. The word has been used by F. W. Chandler and others as a synonym for picaroon. Although the term does emphasize an important aspect of the picaroon's nature, it can also be somewhat misleading, since there is a significant sense, as I shall try to show later, in which the picaresque hero is a genuine hero.

7. The author of *Lazarillo* plays here with the popular kenning for bread, *cara de Dios* (God's face, or presence). See note by J. E. V. Crofts in *Lazarillo,* p. 77.

8. *Ibid.,* p. 21.

9. *Ibid.,* p. 29.

10. Rowland inserts "by chance" twice in this sentence, but the original text ascribes only the tinker's arrival to *acaso,* not the master's departure as well.

11. *Lazarillo,* p. 11.

12. *Ibid.,* p. 46.

13. Rowland omits the bracketed phrase, which appears in the original.

II. THE INCORRUPTIBILITY OF THE PICARESQUE HERO

1. Alain-René Lesage, *Histoire de Gil Blas de Santillane*, ed. Maurice Bardon (2 vols.; Paris: Editions Garnier Frères, 1955), II, 88. All citations are from this edition.

2. All translations of foreign-language quotations are my own.

3. I, 44.

4. See Lanson's article on Lesage in his *Histoire Illustrée de la Littérature Française*, vol. II (Paris: Hachette et Compagnie, 1926), p. 62.

5. I, 66.

6. I, 312.

7. I, 86.

8. Scipion is also the name of one of the canine dialogists in Cervantes' *Colloquy of the Dogs*. The irony of Lesage's novel is similar in temper to that of *The Colloquy:* we sense in both an intimate acquaintance with the ubiquity of human corruption that is marked by neither embitterment nor anger but rather by a kind of detached, good-humored enjoyment in observing the spectacle of universal folly.

9. I, 16.

10. I, 15.

11. I, 17.

12. I, 14.

13. I, 4.

14. I, 84.

15. II, 52.

16. I, 123–126.

17. Claudio Guillén, "The Anatomies of Roguery" (unpub. diss., Harvard University, 1953), p. 440.

18. "Souple jusqu'à la bassesse . . . mais partout et toujours observateur." Eugene Lintilhac, *Lesage* (Paris: Hachette et Compagnie, 1893), p. 110.

19. I, 192. It should be kept in mind that Lesage had an axe to grind against professional actors for the way they dropped his *Turcaret* and that he uses this whole episode to hone that instrument of grudge to a particularly fine edge. In contrast to the vehement disgust Gil Blas shows for theater people, his feelings toward bandits and swindlers seem almost approving.

20. "Gil Blas se moque-t-il de lui-même ou de son inter-locuteur?" I, 383.

21. I, 191.

22. II, 119–120.

23. II, 135.

24. I am indebted here to a suggestion by Professor Herbert Dieckmann.

A BOURGEOIS PICAROON 141

25. Erich Auerbach, *Mimesis: The Representation of Reality in Western Literature*, trans. Willard Trask (Princeton, N.J.: Princeton University Press, 1953), p. 12.
26. Miguel de Cervantes, *Don Quixote de la Mancha*, trans. Thomas Shelton (3 vols.; London: Macmillan and Co., 1908), I, 178.

III. A BOURGEOIS PICAROON

1. Daniel Defoe, *The Fortunes and Misfortunes of the Famous Moll Flanders*, ed. G. H. Maynadier (2 vols.; Boston: The University Press, 1903), I, xvii. All textual references are to this edition.
2. II, 45.
3. I, 131–132.
4. II, 21; I, 233–234; I, 234.
5. I, 244.
6. I, 46–47.
7. I, xx.
8. I, 194; I, 200; II, 33; II, 201.
9. I, 141; I, 105; II, 173
10. *The Merchant of Venice*, I, iii, 23–24; II, iv, 34.
11. I, 36.
12. I, 100.
13. Max Weber, *The Protestant Ethic and the Spirit of Capitalism*, trans. Talcott Parsons (New York: Charles Scribner's Sons, 1958), pp. 18–19, 76.
14. Moll frequently speaks of the noneconomic aspects of her life in the language of the tradesman. She refers to her "stock" of moral qualities and thinks about "increasing her store" of virtue.
15. E. A. Baker, *The History of the English Novel* (9 vols.; London: H. F. and G. Witherly, 1929), III, 190.
16. For Weber's explanation of the traditionalist society as distinguished from modern capitalist society, see his *Protestant Ethic*, pp. 58f.
17. Charles H. and Katherine George, *The Protestant Mind of the English Reformation: 1570–1640*. (Princeton: Princeton University Press, 1961), p. 147.
18. I, 25; I, 28; I, 32.
19. II, 48; II, 86; I, 144.
20. II, 45.
21. I, 193.
22. Ian Watt, *The Rise of the Novel* (Berkeley and Los Angeles: University of California Press, 1957), p. 112.
23. E. M. Forster, *Aspects of the Novel* (New York: Harcourt, Brace, and Co., 1927), pp. 91–92.

24. I, 220.

25. For a concise and lucid discussion of the precapitalist sense of community, see L. C. Knights, *Drama and Society in the Age of Jonson* (London: Chatto and Windus, 1936), pp. 17f.

26. Many rural areas of the American South, at least until fairly recently, embodied one particular variety of this precapitalist sense of community. Faulkner's novel *The Hamlet* presents a vivid picture of a capitalist ethic encroaching upon Southern traditionalism. Flem Snopes, with all his hard-eyed, fast-dealing kinsmen, moves in on the sleepy townlet of Frenchman's Bend. The old sense of social and economic community, most strikingly represented by V. K. Ratliff, easy-going itinerant sewing machine salesman and cousin to everyone, yields to the aggressive enterprise of the Snopeses, a clan in which the closest blood cousins would not dare trust one another.

27. Weber, *Protestant Ethic*, p. 51.

28. *Ibid.*, p. 53.

29. This is why Moll, after one successful attempt at the gaming table (frequently a favorite place for picaresque diversion), vows never to gamble again. She does not object to robbery since it is a surer kind of venture, but gambling must be avoided as a deadly sin because it involves a very high risk of good capital.

30. II, 101; II, 109.

31. II, 173; II, 209–210.

32. II, 117–118.

33. Balzac's *César Birotteau* makes painfully clear what a dismal fate bankruptcy is for the entrepreneur. As Birotteau's grandeur and decline indicate, the social disgrace of bankruptcy is in itself an agonizing "punishment" for that deadly sin, even without a prison sentence.

34. II, 117; I, 248; I, 147.

35. Virginia Woolf, *The Common Reader* (London: Hogarth Press, 1929), pp. 130–131.

36. Henry Peacham, *The Worth of a Peny or a Caution to Keep Money* (London: privately printed, 1647), p. 15.

37. See Weber, *Protestant Ethic*, pp. 162f.

38. II, 211–212.

IV. THE PICAROON AS FORTUNE'S PLAYTHING

1. Tobias Smollett, *Peregrine Pickle*, ed. G. H. Maynadier (3 vols.; Cambridge, Mass.: The University Press, 1903), III, 16.

2. Tobias Smollett, *The Adventures of Roderick Random*, ed.

G. H. Maynadier (3 vols.; Cambridge, Mass.: The University Press, 1902), I, xxxi–xxxii. All textual references are to this edition.

3. I, xxxii.

4. I, xxxii.

5. J. H. Plumb, *England in the Eighteenth Century* (Penguin Books, No. A231; London: Penguin Books, Ltd., 1950), p. 12.

6. *Ibid.*, p. 95.

7. Ronald Paulson, "Satire in the Early Novels of Smollett," *Journal of English and Germanic Philology*, 59 (1960), 381–402.

8. I, 10.

9. II, 70.

10. Such helplessness in the face of coldly inhuman cruelty is reproduced with terrifying effect when Melville undertakes an imitation of Smollett in the death's-head surgeon of *White-Jacket*, Cadwallader Cuticle. Melville's novel makes explicit what can be inferred from Smollett's: that the ship is a microcosm and that, consequently, the arbitrary power of the ship's officers is all the more maddening because, within the world created in the novel, no imaginable limits can be imposed on it.

11. I, 11.

12. I, 137.

13. I, 198; II, 161.

14. I, 220.

15. I, 29–30.

16. II, 33.

17. Americo Castro has observed that the picaresque novel from its inception creates a peculiar sense that "reality is only the appearance of reality, a make-believe sustained by craft and knavery." See his introduction to *Lazarillo de Tormes* (Madison, Wis.: University of Wisconsin Press, 1948), p. xii. Dickens, who began his career in the picaresque tradition, and who was from boyhood an avid admirer of Smollett, both imitated and surpassed the Scottish writer in the use of caricature in fiction; and critics have often spoken of a quality of "sur-reality" in Dickens' novels.

18. II, 133; I, 192.

19. I assume that every coherent social grouping holds some belief or beliefs in common, at least tacitly. These beliefs, of course, need not be traditional religious dogmas. In the case of a society characterized by acquisitive capitalism, the common, reassuring belief would be the conviction that accumulation of wealth is the one significant human activity.

20. Writers of the eighteenth century, living in a thoroughly postheroic age, often show an awareness of such dubious re-

incarnations of the traditional hero, or are even led to look on heroism in general with a jaundiced eye. Compare Fielding's treatment of "greatness" in *Jonathan Wild* and Swift's idea in *A Tale of a Tub,* Section IX, of the hero as a mere madman whose madness coincides with historical necessity.

21. "The Jew felt his own life as an example of the conflict between the total personality and its environment, between the consciousness of its own worth and society's resistance against recognizing it." Americo Castro, *The Structure of Spanish History* (Princeton: Princeton University Press, 1954), p. 557. Castro reminds us (p. 558, note) that the authors of both *Guzman de Alfarache* and *Celestina* were of Jewish origin, and concludes that *Lazarillo* is also the work of a convert or a Jew. See also p. 599, note.

22. Smollett, *Letters,* ed. E. S. Noyes (Cambridge, Mass.: Harvard University Press, 1926), pp. 69–70.

23. III, 96. For a lucid and persuasive analysis of Smollett's stylistic limitations, see Albrecht Strauss's excellent article "On Smollett's Language" in *Style in Prose Fiction,* ed. Harold C. Martin (New York: Columbia University Press, 1959), pp. 25–54.

24. This underlying unity in Smollett's method of description was called to my attention by Arthur Gold.

25. III, 130. Compare Ian Watt on Fielding in *The Rise of the Novel,* p. 274.

26. II, 229.

27. III, 243.

28. Auerbach, *Mimesis,* pp. 397–398.

29. There is a distinction, of course, between sensibility and sentimentalism. Sensibility is the term usually attached to the cult of feeling that flourished in the last decades of the eighteenth century, while sentimentalism is a tendency that is present in all ages. But the two attitudes—the overvaluing of the emotions and the insistence on the ubiquity and importance of certain emotional responses—are related. They appear in *Roderick Random* as part of a single complex, and for that reason I felt justified in discussing them here under the same heading.

V. THE PICAROON DOMESTICATED

1. The most noteworthy performance of this sort in recent years is in Ian Watt's *The Rise of the Novel.*

2. Henry Fielding, *The History of Tom Jones. A Foundling,* introduction by George Sherborn (Modern Library No. 185; New York: Random House, 1950), pp. 423–424. All textual references are to this edition.

3. Cf. Watt, *The Rise of the Novel,* p. 15.

4. An epigrammist like Gil Blas is a limited exception to this rule.

5. Page 77.

6. Page 319.

7. Page 270.

8. Third page of introduction, unpaginated.

9. Page 560.

10. Henry Fielding, *Joseph Andrews*, ed. Maynard Mack (Rinehart Editions, No. 15; New York; Rinehart and Co., 1948), p. xxi.

11. Since the advent of New Criticism, the meaning of the term irony has been stretched till it is sometimes almost unrecognizable. An intelligent reconsideration of the term is Eleanor N. Hutchens' "The Identification of Irony" in *ELH*, 27 (1960): 352–363. Miss Hutchens defines irony as "the sport of bringing about a conclusion by indicating its opposite." She calls it a "sport" because irony, in distinction, for example, to military ruse, is not meant to achieve an immediate practical end; it is engaged in for its own sake.

12. All the uses cited by the Oxford English Dictionary for predicament in the sense of state of being, from 1586 on, have the negative implication.

13. A. R. Humphreys, "Fielding's Irony: Its Methods and Effects," *Review of English Studies*, 18 (1942): 183.

14. Joshua Reynolds, *Discourses on Art* (San Marino, Calif.: Huntington Library, 1959), p. 107.

15. José Ortega y Gasset, "Notes on the Novel" in *The Dehumanization of Art and Other Writings on Art and Culture* (Anchor Books, No. A72; Garden City, N.Y.: Doubleday and Co., 1956), p. 54.

VI. HEIRS OF THE TRADITION

1. Northrop Frye, *Anatomy of Criticism* (Princeton: Princeton University Press, 1957). See especially pp. 304–310.

2. André Gide, *Interviews Imaginaires* (New York: Pantheon Press, 1943), Interviews VIII and IX.

3. Thomas Hardy, quoted by Florence Emily Hardy in *The Later Years of Thomas Hardy* (New York: The Macmillan Company, 1930), p. 44.

4. "Un roman: c'est un miroir qu'on promène le long d'un chemin." Stendhal (Henri Beyle), *Le Rouge et le Noir, Chronique du XIXe Siècle*, ed. Henri Martineau (Bourges, France: Editions Garnier Frères, 1960), p. 76.

5. *Ibid.*, p. 62.

6. *Ibid.*, p. 275.

7. *Ibid.*, p. 324.

146 NOTES TO CHAPTER VI

8. *Ibid.*, p. 303.
9. See J. Y. T. Grieg, *Thackeray, A Reconsideration* (London: Oxford University Press, 1950), pp. 96–98.
10. William Makepeace Thackeray, *The Memoirs of Barry Lyndon, Esq.* (New York: Charles Scribner's Sons, 1904), p. 279.
11. *Ibid.*, pp. 177, 330, 60.
12. Walter Allen, *The English Novel* (New York: E. P. Dutton and Co., 1954), p. 193. Mr. Allen makes this observation in connection with Dickens, and Dickens' own laments on the replacement of the stagecoach by the railroad are relevant here. There are marked picaresque elements in Dickens, particularly early in his career, beginning notably with Alfred Jingle, Esq. But the author of *Pickwick* felt himself circumscribed by the rapidly growing machine age; partly because of it he was led gradually to change his novelistic method.
13. Thackeray, p. 112.
14. Wallace Stegner, introduction to *The Adventures of Huckleberry Finn* (Laurel Editions; New York: Dell Publishing Co., 1960), p. 10.
15. Mark Twain (Samuel Clemens), *The Adventures of Huckleberry Finn*, introduction by Wallace Stegner (Laurel Editions: New York: Dell Publishing Co., 1960), pp. 103, 105.
16. *Ibid.*, p. 147.
17. *Ibid.*, p. 25.
18. Saul Bellow, *The Adventures of Augie March* (New York: The Viking Press, 1960), p. 3.
19. *Ibid.*, p. 32.
20. *Ibid.*, p. 95.
21. *Ibid.*, pp. 84–85.
22. *Ibid.*, p. 151.
23. *Ibid.*, p. 485.
24. *Ibid.*, pp. 454, 523.
25. *Ibid.*, p. 536.
26. Thomas Mann, *Gesammelte Werke*, vol. VII: *Bekenntnisse des Hochstaplers Felix Krull* (Oldenburg, Germany: S. Fischer Verlag, 1960), pp. 417, 331.
27. *Ibid.*, p. 491.
28. *Ibid.*, p. 503.
29. Joyce Cary, *The Horse's Mouth* (New York: Harper and Brothers, 1944), p. 111.
30. *Ibid.*, p. 174.
31. *Ibid.*, p. 299.
32. *Ibid.*, p. 1.
33. *Ibid.*, p. 311.

INDEX

HARVARD STUDIES IN
COMPARATIVE LITERATURE